Kant and Liberal Internationalism

Sovereignty, Justice, and Global Reform

BY

Antonio Franceschet

palgrave
macmillan

First published 2002 by
PALGRAVE MACMILLAN™
175 Fifth Avenue, New York, N.Y. 10010 and
Houndmills, Basingstoke, Hampshire, England RG21 6XS
Companies and representatives throughout the world

PALGRAVE MACMILLAN is the global academic imprint of the Palgrave Macmillan division of St. Martin's Press, LLC and of Palgrave Macmillan Ltd. Macmillan® is a registered trademark in the United States, United Kingdom and other countries. Palgrave is a registered trademark in the European Union and other countries.

ISBN 0–312–29617–7

Library of Congress Cataloging-in-Publication Data
Franceschet, Antonio.
    Kant and liberal internationalism : sovereignty, justice, and global reform/Antonio Franceschet.
        p. cm.
    Includes bibliographical references and index.
    ISBN 0–312–29617–7
        1. International relations—Philosophy. 2. Kant, Immanuel, 1724–1804—Views on international relations. 3. Sovereignty. 4. Justice. 5. Internationalism. I. Title.

JZ1306.F73 2002
327.1'7—dc 21   2002068406

A catalogue record for this book is available from the British Library.

Design by Newgen Imaging Systems (P) Ltd., Chennai, India.

First edition: October, 2002
10 9 8 7 6 5 4 3 2 1

Printed in the United States of America.

FOR SUSAN

CONTENTS

ABBREVIATIONS FOR
KANT'S WORKS

C.Pur refers to *Critique of Pure Reason,* trans. Werner S. Pluhar. Indianapolis and Cambridge: Hackett Publishing Company Inc., 1996.

C.Pr refers to *Critique of Practical Reason,* trans. Lewis White Beck. Saddle River, New Jersey: Prentice Hall/Library of Liberal Arts, 1993.

CJ refers to *Critique of Judgment,* trans. Werner S. Pluhar. Indianapolis and Cambridge: Hackett Publishing Company Inc., 1987.

GMM refers to *Groundwork of the Metaphysic of Morals,* trans. H. J. Paton. New York: Harpertorch Books, 1964.

MM refers to *The Metaphysics of Morals,* trans. Mary Gregor. Cambridge: Cambridge University Press, 1996.

REL refers to *Religion in the Limits of Reason Alone,* trans. T. M. Greene and H. H. Hudson. New York: Harper & Row, 1960.

UH refers to "Idea for a Universal History with a Cosmopolitan Purpose," in *Kant: Political Writings,* ed. Hans Reiss and trans. H. B. Nisbet. Cambridge: Cambridge University Press, 1991.

QE refers to "An Answer to the Question: 'What Is Enlightenment?' " in *Kant: Political Writings,* op. cit.

TP refers to "On the Common Saying: 'This May Be True in Theory, but It Does Not Apply in Practice,' " in *Kant: Political Writings,* op. cit.

PP refers to "Perpetual Peace: A Philosophical Sketch," in *Kant: Political Writings,* op. cit.

CF refers to "The Contest of the Faculties," in *Kant: Political Writings,* op. cit.

CBH refers to "Conjectures on the Beginning of Human History," in *Kant: Political Writings,* op. cit.

References to C.Pur, C.Pr, and MM cite first the Academy pagination followed by the page number of the specific translations used.

Preface and Acknowledgments

Since the rise of the modern state system there have been many proposals for its reform. This book is concerned with the nature of, and relationship between, two specific cases of the desire to progressively alter the nature of international politics, one philosophical and the other ideological. In 1795, Immanuel Kant first published "Perpetual Peace," an essay that offers a series of philosophical claims about the necessity and possibility of rendering the relations among sovereign states more peaceful, just, and—ultimately—compatible with the freedom of human beings. Since that time, Kant's claims have often been appropriated by liberal ideology—an ideology that, when applied to the relations among states, also aims to explain why international reform is necessary, in addition to prescribing what individuals, peoples, and governments must do to attain it. This diverse body of ideas is known as "liberal internationalism."

Any desire to reform international politics presupposes certain things about human beings, political societies, sovereign states, and the type of interactions that generally occur among them. In the case of Kant, a complex "critical" philosophical system is the foundation by which he justifies why, and explains how, a change in the putative nature of international politics is required. This book aims to explain Kant's conclusions and, further, to speculate why his particular answers to the twin problems of war and injustice have been so popular yet so difficult to interpret equivocally.

Interpreting Kant's meaning is important because his legacy has been central and yet ambiguous within the context of an evolving liberal internationalist tradition—a tradition that has become revitalized, if not hegemonic, since the end of the Cold War. A recent renaissance of liberalism has led many scholars in the field of International Relations to look to the past for "founding fathers" of the vision of a more peaceful and more just world order. Even though Kant has been invoked as such a foundation, it is, ultimately, impossible to perceive a coherent or unified intellectual and ideological product; this is because contemporary liberals are divided on the very same political and ethical conundrums on which Kant's texts are, I think, unable to render decisive judgments. Accordingly, this book also forwards reasons why the renewed interest in Kant in recent years has only exacerbated—rather than conclusively settled—a series of preexisting tensions within liberal internationalism, tensions that will likely grow more salient in the future. Although I see liberalism as an inherently crisis-prone ideology, many of its core political commitments can and should be reconstructed to reform and transform today's global order. A central element of this reconstruction is the cosmopolitical democratization of the emerging institutions of global governance.

There have been many previous efforts to interpret Kant's international theory, many of which reflect upon the tendency of other scholars to misinterpret his meaning. The best of these interpretations recognize both that Kant's thoughts on international relations cannot be viewed independently of his larger "critical" system and that, ultimately, this system is fraught with paradoxes and dualities that do not necessarily cohere with existing approaches and paradigms in International Relations. The aim of this book is not merely to rehearse these two points with which I largely agree. Rather, it is to argue something specific about the nature of Kant's international thought and the limitations and possibilities it has created for a distinctly liberal ideological tradition of international theory. Central to this argument is the claim that Kant's international reform project is shaped by his vision of justice. However, his view of justice is only partially and schematically articulated in "Perpetual Peace," and, as a result, far too many scholars have attempted to give an account of this reform project without recognizing its inherent dependence on the problematic nature of Kantian justice. It is, I advance, the most disconcerting feature of his theory of justice—a deeply entrenched if not dogmatic commitment to sovereignty—that renders his legacy difficult to accept without substantial modification. The nature of this modification is not, however, a foregone conclusion. If liberals are to convincingly articulate the required principles and mechanisms of progressive political reform in today's world—and I think that, in principle, they must—a critical debate aimed at rethinking state sovereignty is required. Such a debate may indeed fruitfully draw on certain aspects of Kant's legacy of reform, but it must at a minimum start with an awareness of the crippling limitations that his theory of justice imposes upon his relevance as an intellectual foundation. These limitations, I submit, are particularly significant in light of the globalizing nature of politics, in which progressive and just transformation ought to be conceived in global, rather than the traditionally interstate, terms.

This book is a significantly amended version of the doctoral dissertation that I defended at Carleton University in Ottawa, Canada, May 1999.

In writing, rewriting, and editing it for publication I have accumulated many debts.

David Long supervised the writing of the dissertation with good humor, sage advice, and healthy skepticism. Tom Darby and John Sigler each took great interest in my progress and read the various chapters with care and sound suggestions. James Graff and Howard Williams raised important interpretive and substantive issues at stake in my analysis of Kant and international justice that enriched my perspective and hopefully, this book. The late Pierre Laberge shared some of his vast knowledge of Kant with me at the very early stages of this project—his kindness and humility have formed a lasting memory of a truly generous scholar. W. Andy Knight and Tom Keating read and criticized key portions of this manuscript prepared while I was fortunate to be a Grant Notley Postdoctoral Fellow in Political Science at the University of Alberta.

The Social Sciences and Humanities Research Council of Canada provided a fellowship that funded the initial work on this project.

Thanks are also due to David Pervin for taking an interest in this book and helping make it possible at Palgrave Macmillan.

My greatest debt is to Susan Franceschet for helping to sustain my confidence throughout the years of study, thinking, and writing, and more significantly, for critically reading the results over and over again.

The following permissions are gratefully acknowledged: Select portions of chapters 2, 3, and 4 of this book are drawn from Antonio Franceschet, "Sovereignty and Freedom: Immanuel Kant's Liberal Internationalist 'Legacy,'" *Review of International Studies* 27(2): 209–228, Cambridge University Press, © 2001 British International Studies Association. Select paragraphs of chapter 4 are reprinted with permission from Antonio Franceschet, "The Ethical Foundations of Liberal Internationalism," from *International Journal* 54(3), 1999. Chapter 5 is adapted from Antonio Franceschet, "Justice and International Organization: Two Models of Global Governance," from *Global Governance: A Review of Multilateralism and International Organizations* 8(1), © 2002 by Lynne Rienner Publishers, used with permission. Chapter 6 is reprinted by permission of Sage Publications Ltd. from Antonio Franceschet, "Popular Sovereignty or Cosmopolitan Democracy: Liberalism, Kant and International Reform," *European Journal of International Relations* 6(2): 277–302, © Sage Publications Ltd. and the EPCR European Consortium for Political Research 2000.

INTRODUCTION

Liberals disagree on the nature and purposes of reforming politics. This applies not simply to politics within states and societies but among and across them. Certainly there has always been disagreement in the history of liberalism on the "international problem," that is, anarchy, hostility, and war among states. However, this disagreement is much more profound and important than is conventionally thought. This is because the divisions within liberalism and its internationalist form are exacerbated and complicated by recent global developments and changes. A traditional concern with how best to manage and improve relations among states is now being challenged and is in crisis.[1] There is a growing sense—among some at least—that it is time to go beyond this limited, statist agenda and instead reform and transform a far wider array of political relationships among a plurality of actors, state and nonstate, public and private, national, regional, and local. In short, what is needed is not mere *international* reform but a *global* reform project aimed at democratizing the emerging structures, processes, and institutions of global governance.

The burden of this book is to demonstrate that Immanuel Kant's political philosophy, and the vision of political reform that emerges from it, contributes to our understanding of why traditional liberal internationalism is fundamentally and foundationally limited, in addition to the reasons this tradition can and ought to be restructured. This restructuring of the fundamental attributes and aims of liberal internationalism is, I submit, consistent with the inner ethico-political purposes of liberalism as an ideology dedicated to autonomy and justice. But before these substantive arguments about liberalism and Kant and the relationship between them are unpacked, three developments in recent years need to be emphasized. These changes of context point to the interconnections among political and economic transformation, ideology, history, and the (inevitably normative) theoretical tools we use to explain and understand politics, particularly international and global politics.

The first change regards the *nature* of international politics. The end of the Cold War has given hope to reviving collective security, the

United Nations, and international law as ways of resolving conflicts among states.[2] This hope has long been associated with liberalism. From about the same time, a wave of democratization and redemocratization in Eastern Europe, Latin America, and elsewhere in the global South has occurred.[3] Moreover, a commitment to so-called open economies has been maintained if not strengthened in every corner of the world—and the institutions to facilitate it, such as the World Trade Organization and, regionally, the European Union and the North American Free Trade Agreement, have made advances. From these events, too, a hope long associated with liberalism has been renewed, that is, that states will cooperate to advance the material and the moral interests of the populations to which they are accountable; and further, that states will face irresistible economic incentives to foster and maintain peaceful relations.

A more profound change is in the nature of global politics through globalization. Individual, state, and nonstate actors are growing far more aware of the global nature of all politics since the end of the Cold War. But globalization does not inherently fulfill liberal plans and goals, at least not exclusively. Although the global market economy is perhaps the most obvious manifestation of growing interconnections between all states and societies, it is a process that no one group, society, or state controls.[4] Nor is it a process that is, by any stretch of the imagination, democratically accountable and subject to fundamental principles of justice.[5] Additionally, globalization processes stimulate and provoke nationalism and fundamentalist identities that resist the integration and interpenetration of states and societies, often with clearly illiberal means and purposes.

A second set of changes is in the prevailing ideological precepts that organize the understanding of international and global phenomena and justify the activities of individuals, governments, and other collective identities not reducible to them. The Cold War was arguably an ideological phenomenon foremost, and with the renunciation of communism and apparent decline of socialism, it has been liberalism that has, so to speak, capitalized. Even though the entire planet has not—contrary to Francis Fukuyama's wishes—uniformly embraced liberalism, it has become by the new millennium *the* hegemonic standard against which other modes of governance are judged as lacking.[6] As noted, this tendency applies to interstate affairs: Liberal principles have become increasingly invoked as the most appropriate for explaining relations among states and the dynamics and institutions that shape their interactions.[7] This is so in spite of the fact that these principles are not always adhered to, even by Western liberal democracies. Nevertheless, as this book will show, the use of the "liberal" label is inherently contentious: This ideology has not remained stable in time because it is not monolithic, not least in international and global politics.[8]

A third set of changes concerns the dominant theoretical assumptions and categories peculiar to the discipline of International Relations. Changing political realities and ideological trends are obvious causes of theoretical evolution. According to the well-worn myths of the discipline, however, liberal internationalist ideals are a part of the past.[9] The vision of a progressive transformation of international politics toward a more peaceful and just world order had been defeated and discredited since the mid-1940s. The Cold War sustained an alternative theoretical school, realism, that allegedly defeated liberal internationalism. However, when the Cold War ended, the declining appeal of realism as an explanatory and justificatory theory of international politics suffered. It no longer seemed so "utopian" that power politics could be superseded among states by shared international norms and practices based on common ethical principles and expectations.

For these three general reasons, something remarkable has occurred after the Cold War: All too suddenly, and without much reflection on the historicity of liberal internationalism, important scholars have claimed that liberal ideas were all along superior, or at least had sudden new relevance. For support, they have invoked the names of prestigious philosophers. The most prestigious, it seems, has been the eighteenth-century Prussian Kant. Although the thoughts of Kant appear to have taken on a new relevance, this recycling of venerable formulations of international reform from as long ago as two hundred years does not, I think, necessarily explain, justify, or give us adequate guidance to deal with the challenges and dilemmas of the post-Cold War order. Indeed, it is my perception of a gap between the so-called foundational and traditional formulations of liberal internationalism and the possible requirements of contemporary political reform that has inspired the present book. It is puzzling that, in seeking to answer the ultimately normative question "How ought global politics be conducted or organized?" we should look to the responses of thinkers from very different historical situations than our own. It is remarkable because we often do so in ways that reveal more about our perceptions and prejudices than about what "founding fathers" like Kant actually wrote.[10]

It is in this context that the present book aims to explain Kant's international political theory and its influential connection with liberal internationalism. His theory is premised on a particular view of the relationships among human freedom, state sovereignty, and justice. For Kant, international reform is fundamental to implementing justice *qua* justice in a world populated by essentially finite human beings and imperfect sovereign states. However, a profound difficulty with Kant's theory concerns the fundamental *nature* of justice that he thinks necessary to implement at the global level. Quite simply, Kant is ambiguous or sufficiently vague to have left a divided intellectual and political legacy—a legacy that has been especially important to a subsequent tradition of liberalism. I claim that Kant's ambiguities are twofold because:

- it is unclear whether his conception of individual freedom (which is the ultimate purpose of justice) is a mere *negative* good or should be understood as a *positive* ideal against which human autonomy must be directly and purposively promoted by political institutions;
- it is also controversial whether his advocacy of international reform assumes that it is ultimately or primarily sovereign states or individual beings that are the true subjects of global justice.

This book claims that Kant's political theory is, on balance, a fundamentally limited basis for contemporary and future liberal internationalist reform because it does not provide adequate theoretical support for realizing individual autonomy and global justice in an era of globalization. Although ambiguous, Kant's texts contain a deep-seated bias in favor of a truncated form of negative, libertarian freedom that is restricted by an excessively formal conception of political justice. Moreover, Kant's political theory and its normative explanation of international reform rely on a dogmatic conception of state sovereignty that unnecessarily blunts the force of his cosmopolitanism. Both of these difficulties arise from the deepest ontological and epistemological foundations of his critical project: a set of assumptions and commitments about the nature of morality and politics and their inherent incompatibility.

In spite of these findings, I maintain that Kant is relevant and crucial to understanding international politics and the ways in which it can and ought to be transformed. That is, the textual evidence suggests that Kant had a very narrow and overly statist understanding of reform. But there is always the possibility of reinterpreting and reconstructing Kant's meaning. His most compelling insights can be transformed to fit better the needs of contemporary global justice. Such a recasting of Kantian political theory is not only legitimate but also highly defensible because of the open nature of his philosophical enterprise. That is, Kant's word on his own politics is not final, but instead amenable to new formulations because of the very unstable nature of the dualities and reconciliations upon which his critical philosophy relies.[11] In spite of the limitations of Kant's political posture toward international reform, the two ambiguities I note above concerning freedom, the role of sovereignty, and justice are not ultimately resolved by his own statements in "Perpetual Peace" and elsewhere.[12] In the final analysis, I show that Kantian international reform is shaped jointly by politically "conservative" and "radical" assumptions about sovereign states and the institutionalization of just political relations within and among them.

Using Kant as a model, the book also explains and evaluates the ideological character and limits of mainstream liberal international theory. The open and unfixed nature of Kant's political philosophy is important to explaining his mixed and contradictory appropriation by various liberal political theorists and International Relations scholars. Kant's legacy is thus not a neutral ground or foundation that serves merely as an authoritative source of truth, but is instead an evolving tradition from which competing liberals have drawn and continue to draw inspiration. Nonetheless, I also aim to show that liberal-minded advocates of international political reform are misguided if they follow too closely, implicitly or explicitly, Kant's own limited remedies and prescriptions for international anarchy. The acceptance of the given parameters of "Perpetual Peace," and the theory of political justice upon which it relies, leads to a "classical" liberal internationalism. This classical form of the tradition tends to subordinate individual autonomy to the discretion of sovereign states, the constraints of the international system, and (in some cases) the (neoliberal) global economy. The present argument claims that a reconstructed liberal internationalism is possible if liberals match the underlying cosmopolitan morality that Kant arguably limits and represses with a new understanding of cosmopolitical organization and democratic global governance.[13]

A Note on Method and Structure

This book produces a reconstruction of the foundations of Kant's political philosophy and an interpretation of its intellectual and ideological relationships to liberal internationalism. Compared with other analyses of Kant's texts, my reconstruction of his meaning will appear to some as remarkably "statist" and noncosmopolitan. As will become apparent, this is not a consequence of my ideological or normative convictions; it is instead a reflection of the subject matter and the method that I think is appropriate for such a project. If there is relatively little that is cosmopolitical in my reading of Kant's texts it is because I have subordinated my interpretation of "Perpetual Peace" to his account of justice (principally in the first part of his last major work, the "Doctrine of Right" in the *Metaphysics of Morals*). Indeed, it is only when *The Metaphysics of Morals* is ignored that Kant is (mistakenly) read as a "revolutionary" thinker.[14]

My reconstruction follows the example, if not exact path, of two important Kant scholars, Thomas W. Pogge and Pierre Laberge. Both have paid special attention to the nature of Kantian justice expressed in Kant's statements about the interrelation of morals and politics in *The Metaphysics of Morals*. In assuming this path, I find a "disclaimer" by Pogge to be particularly germane and worth reproducing in this book:

> Being a reconstruction of Kant's own position, the theory I shall sketch out is not as progressive as many of his recent followers would like. But no purpose is served by torturing Kant's own work until it matches what we now view as the most reasonable Kantian theory of justice for our time.[15]

Laberge, too, has written about Kant's theory of justice and has been one of the few to apply it clearly and explicitly to the question of international reform.[16] Like Pogge, Laberge characterizes Kantian justice as being doggedly formal and thus essentially "progressive-conservative" rather than revolutionary. Indeed, if we consider faithfully the nature of the limits that Kant imposes upon all political reform, some disturbingly "illiberal" undercurrents of his statism become apparent. As Pogge and Laberge have shown, it is only by ignoring Kant's robust (if not "dogmatic") commitment to sovereignty that it is possible to construct an antistatist, revolutionary cosmopolitanism out of his legacy.[17]

Nonetheless, the present reconstruction of Kant's political and international theory has two distinct features. First, I develop a conceptual framework for interpreting Kant's meaning that transcends the literal precepts of Kantian justice. This means that, in contrast with Laberge for example, I do not simply recapitulate Kant's statements on justice and international justice in order to dispel misinterpretation. As Fernando R. Tesón notes, Laberge's work is powerful but still limited to exegesis rather than reconstructive interpretation: "The difference is important, because the reconstructive approach implies sometimes disagreeing with the philosopher and improving upon his or her arguments."[18] Laberge thus accepts all too faithfully the authority of Kant on international politics, to the point that he duplicates rather than challenges its problematic facets. I thus ultimately follow more closely Pogge and attempt to explain critically how and why Kant arrived at the limited vision of international justice that he did.

Second, I place Kantian justice within two distinct contexts, one philosophic and the other ideological. My reconstruction considers firstly how this justice emerges from Kant's "critical" reaction to modernity and the problem of individual subjectivity. Kant's justification of sovereignty is, I show, an attempt to reconcile politics with what he views as the only plausibly solid ground of the modern subject: an autonomous morality. I also demonstrate that Kant's (eventually limited) critique of state sovereignty and his project to reform it are inherent parts of the same quest to domesticate politics through formal principles derived from morality. The other context in which I place Kantian justice is the continuing evolution of liberal internationalism. Kant's plans to reform international politics for the sake of freedom and justice clearly make his thought compatible with this ideology. However, I show that the underlying foundations of his thought render a Kantian legacy within this tradition unstable and open to varying ideological interpretations.

The first three chapters explain the genesis, justification, and nature of Kant's international reform project. Chapter 1 explains why his "critical" philosophy is motivated by his unique quest to subordinate politics to an autonomous morality (i.e., the categorical imperative). I argue that Kant's critique of previous modern discourses of politics ultimately leads him to accept a deep separation of politics and morals. This bifurcation of politics and morals is the ontological foundation of his international reform project. Chapter 2 explores the significance of the central concept of freedom in Kant's philosophical system. Kant's assumption about the differences between politics and morals results in his division of freedom into two separate but related spheres, the "internal" and "external." By reconstructing the relationship between these two kinds of freedom, this chapter builds a framework to understand Kantian justice. Justice is necessary *because* of the very gap between the politics and morals that he assumes; and its realization is found in the reform of all political relations, domestic, interstate, and—to a limited degree—from a cosmopolitan point of view.

A theory of justice requires an account of political agents and their attendant rights and duties in society and even in international society. In chapter 3 I draw out the salient and controversial elements of Kantian justice that explain his perpetual peace project. In particular, Kant's account of justice is conditioned by a strong apology for the sovereign state as the ultimate mechanism through which liberal-style rights and duties are produced. However, this chapter also shows that Kant is aware that a purely "domestic" justice regime is problematic: The mere existence of sovereign states necessarily creates injustice among states and, moreover, threatens the perfection of justice domestically. Kant thus proposes international reform in a way that inspires "classical" liberal internationalism: The promotion of peace and (the duty of) nonintervention allow the reconciliation of internal and external sovereignty in a way that maximizes formal justice. The chapter additionally demonstrates that Kant's justification for international reform is extremely ambiguous because, on the one hand, his project suggests that states are the essential subjects of international justice; and on the other, his deeper moral justification of international reform assumes that states are merely practical tools to be evaluated solely by their capacity to promote the ends of the true subjects of justice, individuals.

Chapters 4 through 6 assess the complex influence of Kant's legacy in the broader tradition of liberal internationalism. Kant's texts do not buttress a coherent tradition of liberal reform—but serve as a divided foundation for the divergent perceptions of liberals about how and why international peace and justice can and should be realized. Chapter 4 examines the ideological substance of liberal internationalism and locates Kant's place within it. Divisions among internationalists are a result of divergent perceptions of the ethical capacities of sovereign states as agents of just political transformation. Kant's international thought contains philosophical materials for two liberal legacies, a "classical" and statist liberal internationalism and a more "radical," cosmopolitan poststatism. In chapter 5, elements of Kant's legacy guide my analysis of the current "crisis of liberal internationalism" that is a result of *inter alia* globalization processes. This crisis is not simply, as Stanley Hoffmann claims, a function of declining state capacities in the face of post-Cold War tribal nationalisms and neoliberal global markets. It is, rather more specifically, a consequence of the weakness and closed nature of existing international institutions in the face of justice claims beyond those of sovereign states. Chapter 6 examines critically two recent liberal research programs with distinct visions of reform based on divergent internationalist ethical concerns and strategies. These two visions—the "democratic peace" thesis and the "cosmopolitan democracy" model—explicitly rely on contrasting Kantian legacies. In comparing these contemporary liberal visions of reform, two arguments are made: First, both democratic peace theorists and cosmopolitan democracy proponents construct their Kantian foundations from distinct, partial, and often unacknowledged assumptions about the actual nature of his theory of justice. Second, in spite of certain weaknesses, cosmopolitan democracy is a superior vision of reform in the contemporary world and a more plausible basis for a reconstructed liberal internationalism. This is because, unlike the democratic peace approach, the cosmopolitan democracy model does not rely upon problematic notions of popular sovereignty as the exclusive basis of grounding justice in today's world. The conclusion of the book examines how and why a reconstruction of Kant's legacy is possible and desirable.

CHAPTER 1

THE FOUNDATIONS OF KANT'S
REFORM PROJECT: POLITICS AND
MORALS

> Two things fill the mind with ever new and increasing admiration and awe, the oftener and more steady they are reflected on: the starry heavens above me and the moral law within me.
>
> —Kant[1]

The wonder expressed in this statement is the inspiration of Kant's critical philosophy. This "awe" is explicitly divided here by the two distinct forces that, when subjected to his scrutiny, form the main elements of a unique political philosophy. The individual occupies a special place in the cosmos because he or she is both a finite being that is determined by the laws of nature and a subject of the supersensible moral law. However, whereas the laws of nature are mechanical and cannot respect any phenomena or beings as ends, the moral law obligates human subjects to act on principles that enshrine men and women as dignified ends.

The dualism expressed by this ontology pervades all of Kant's thinking, including his vision of politics and the nature of justice. Nature is an ultimate cause of injustice not because we suffer and are always left unsatisfied by our physical dependence upon its objects; but, rather, it is because this dependence leads us to act on maxims of (self)-interest rather than the moral law that injustice arises. Even more dangerous, if individuals realize that they are but small and inconsequential objects within nature's mechanism, they may no longer conceive of themselves and others as moral subjects. If we are not dignified ends within the causality of nature, why ought we respect each other as worthy of dignity? The problematic of Kant's critical philosophy is, then, to address our dual position as conditioned, finite beings who are perpetually uncertain about the status of the moral principles that our reason prescribes unconditionally.

In this chapter I place Kantian political philosophy within the context of this larger critical system. I claim that his critical political philosophy is motivated by, *inter alia,* the desire to produce the foundations for justice by restricting the scope of nature's laws and, more crucially, revealing the sovereignty of the moral law. Central to this argument is the fact that Kant's critique is aimed at overturning the assumptions of early-modern philosophers regarding individual subjectivity. In Kant's view, previous modern philosophers fail to recognize the inherent dignity of humans because they depict individuals as determined by the mechanism of nature. Although, for example, Newtonian science and Machiavellian politics both purport to promote human supremacy over nature, they only enhance our domination by nature's forces because they portray us as motivated solely by the "amoral" goals of happiness and material satisfaction. The endless quest for scientific knowledge and the imperative of political expediency are shown by Kant to be inadequate depictions of the individual's will. His critical philosophy holds out an alternative ground for human subjectivity. Rather than an autonomous science or an autonomous politics, Kant holds that the ground of subjectivity is an autonomous *morality.* It is thus "duty for its own sake," rather than speculative knowledge or political action, that is the true foundation of human subjectivity and, as I will show, of Kantian justice.

Ultimately, the way in which Kant criticizes early-modern philosophical assumptions has profound consequences for the shape of his political thought. This is because, in locating the supreme grounds of individual subjectivity in the ethereal plane of pure duty, his vision becomes dualistic in a way one might not intuitively expect. That is, although Kant criticizes Machiavelli's separation of politics and ethics, his conception of a sovereign, autonomous morality leads him to do the much the same thing. For Kant's depiction of subjectivity separates (the pure, unconditioned realm of) morality and (the corrupted, conditioned realm of) politics. This peculiarly Kantian alienation of politics from ethics will be shown to have decisive effects on shaping the main elements of his vision of justice. There are two sections in this chapter. The first argues that the genesis of Kantian critique is in a concern for human dignity as the foundation of justice. Here I examine in particular Kant's critique of science because it provides the inspiration for his critical treatment of Machiavellian politics. The second section explains why the categorical imperative is a direct response to early modern philosophy and the cause of a dualistic foundation for Kant's politics, both domestic and international.

THE NATURE OF KANT'S CRITIQUE AND HUMAN DIGNITY

Until rather recently, Kant's philosophy was not generally viewed in terms of his contribution to political and international thought. The emphasis was instead limited to the epistemological revolution contained in the *Critique of Pure Reason* (1781). The context in which Kant's thought was typically discussed was the debate between rationalism and empiricism. From this vantage point, the chief concern of critical philosophy is a defense of reason from David Hume's skeptical assault on the concept of causality. Kant's motives are thus traditionally confined to that of protecting the status of knowledge by, paradoxically, limiting and restricting that which can be coherently known by finite human beings. Although this portrait of the motives of critical philosophy is accurate, it is necessarily incomplete.

A revival of interest in Kant during the later part of the twentieth century has led to a deeper understanding of the political and moral foundations of his philosophy of critique. Kant's motives are not merely to protect and elaborate upon modern metaphysics. Rather, this particular agenda is a subordinate part of a larger task—that of protecting and extending the "rights of man."[2] Kant's resolution of the differences between rationalists and empiricists is thus a component of a broader critique of modernity for failing to recognize and enshrine the true subjectivity of the individual through a concern for moral dignity.

Kant gains his inspiration for this overarching concern with moral dignity from Jean-Jacques Rousseau. Modern thinkers prior to Rousseau assumed that nature was inherently indifferent to human dignity. Early-modern assumptions about subjectivity depend upon the separation of the individual from an alienated, objective natural order that can no longer fulfill his or her material and spiritual needs—at least not without his or her active willing over nature and other beings. Moreover, insofar as individual subjects are thought to be motivated (viz., caused) by natural inclinations they too are indifferent to each other's dignity. In criticizing this early-modern vision of individual subjectivity, Rousseau's two *Discourses* claim that modern science and politics in particular cannot solve the "problem" that he identifies—the restoration of man's natural dignity—for they are actually the twin causes of his corruption.[3] Kant was moved by Rousseau's indictment of modernity. Years before he articulated his critical project, he inscribed the following notation on a copy of his own *Observations on the Feeling of the Beautiful and the Sublime* (1764): "Rousseau set me right."[4] Rousseau prompted Kant to reevaluate and reflect upon his own assumptions about modern science and to become concerned with its impact upon morality and politics.[5] When Kant eventually pronounced his critical philosophy, Rousseau's influence was unmistakable: The requirements of morality necessarily subordinate and determine the boundaries of modern knowledge and political agency.

Despite Kant's overarching view of the need to protect human dignity from an autonomously conceived science and politics, he opts not to follow Rousseau's radical prescriptions for what ails modern humans. Instead, Kant seeks to find a way to preserve and improve upon the accomplishments of modern thought by restoring the force of morality as the ultimate foundation of human subjectivity and, ultimately, his view of justice.[6] Kant's criticism of modernity is thus not a blanket rejection or demolition project. The nature of his critique is first to restrict modern assumptions about the nature of subjectivity—insofar as they impinge upon human dignity—and then to legislate an autonomous *moral* realm that must subordinate both science and politics. In the *Critique of Pure Reason* Kant characterizes this as a "negative" restriction on modern reason's claim to know, and thereby to *condition,* the individual subject.[7] An autonomous scientific knowledge cannot, therefore, constitute the grounds of authentic subjectivity. More crucially, as it is extended in the *Critique of Practical Reason* (1788), Kant's critique of modernity is deeply practical. Political action cannot have its own autonomous logic, as Machiavelli suggests; it too must be subordinated to the requirements of morality.

Reminiscent of Aristotle, Kant states that although there is only one human reason, it has two distinct applications, "theoretical" and "practical."[8] "The theoretical use of reason is concerned with objects of the merely cognitive faculty ... [which is] different from the practical use of reason," which "deals with the grounds determining the will."[9] As with Aristotle, theoretical knowledge pertains to that which cannot change through human volition, while the practical admits of variation because of human agency. Unlike Aristotle, however, Kant associates theoretical and practical reason with radically distinct types of "causality": the natural and the moral. The former pertains to the mechanism of nature, while the latter is the capacity of the individual will to determine itself independently from nature. Kant's philosophy of critique stakes out the limits and possibilities of both forms of reason and the types of causality with which they are associated. The aim is, as noted, to enshrine and thereby to protect human dignity.

THEORETICAL REASON: THE CRITIQUE OF
SUBJECTIVITY AS KNOWING

The *Critique of Pure Reason* gives a paradoxical apology for metaphysics because it is based on a revolutionary rejection of its previously held foundations. A sound basis for knowledge of nature is possible, according to this text, only under the most strict of epistemological limits. The classical view of philosophy—as the (unfulfilled) desire for wisdom—must thus be regulated by agreed-upon rules that prevent reason from falling into contradiction. These limits on the human capacity to *know* are peculiar to modernity because subjects have taken an autonomous stance vis-à-vis nature. The quest for knowledge of natural causality cannot be governed solely by reason's self-generated, internal desire to possess wisdom; for Kant holds that the legitimate condition of reason's autonomy is the recognition of the "constitutional" limits to what it may claim to represent as the truth.[10] These limits on the capacity of modern rational subjects to delve into the prior determining causes of nature, both human and nonhuman, have the moral function of protecting human dignity. As Kant reflects in the Preface, he finds it necessary to "annul *knowledge* in order to make room for *faith*" in the authentic grounds of autonomy.[11]

Kant is reacting to the consequences on modern subjectivity inherent in Newtonian science. Newton reopened the ancient question of causality by proposing that the mathematical deduction of matter in motion could establish that the laws of nature were determined by mechanism (i.e., the "universal machine").[12] This view of the cosmos seemingly extends the sovereignty of humans over nature because, as Francis Bacon for example believed, we could enhance the welfare of the species. By conceiving of nature as a hostile system of material causes that are inherently indifferent to our ends, or to the Good, nature becomes an object of manipulation for whatever smaller ends that individual subjects posit. Informed by this view of subjectivity, modern science assumes the conceit of total autonomy from nature.

To be sure, as Susan Meld Shell notes, "Kant concurred in this scientific understanding of nature."[13] As long as humans are dependent upon nature, Kant thinks they can never mature morally and will always rely upon crude and debased inclinations as the sole motivation of action.[14] But Kant's sympathy with modern science has crucial limits that must also be recognized. This is because, although he too opposes the subject to nature, it is not with the aim of enhancing human welfare or happiness. Instead, Kant thinks that nature cannot inform the grounds of true subjectivity because, when conceived as a mechanism, the individual cannot be coherently represented as a dignified end. The type of independence from nature that Kant's critical philosophy seeks to establish is thus different in kind from other predominant views of modern science. As Shell claims, Kant quickly became disenchanted with this aspect of modernity: "The material comforts which modern science provides … [cannot] compensate for its devastation of our sense of harmony with nature and our feeling of importance within it." As a result, "Kant set himself the difficult task of recovering and reasserting the spiritual assertions which science seemed irrevocably to destroy."[15]

Under the assumptions of modern subjectivity prior to Kant, the quest for scientific knowledge potentially undermines human dignity. If the desire for knowledge of nature's laws is motivated by happiness and material comfort within an alien cosmos, there can be no possible limit to what is transformed by scientific questioning. Material desires are boundless. The boundary that Kant is concerned will be violated by modern science is the dignity of each individual as an end. The problem, thus, is that earlier moderns do not view subjectivity correctly because they do not actually set apart the individual from the mechanism of nature that they have posited. Because humans are viewed solely in terms of the mechanistic workings of their desires, as in the case of Hobbes, Kant fears that individuals become a mere part of the mechanism of nature over which modern science seeks to establish control.[16] An autonomous science is entirely incompatible with true human autonomy, which, as will be claimed below, Kant asserts is the only objective end within nature. Kant's critique of knowledge is thus an attempt to deny that subjectivity can be located merely in the desire to know and tame nature's laws. If this desire is unchecked by the boundary of human dignity, science will indeed be autonomous and individuals will necessarily be reduced to feeble and conditioned subjects, unable to free themselves from the necessity of nature and unable to live by laws that they themselves have legislated. If, as an autonomous science presupposes, human beings are only the products of mechanistic natural laws, they would be unable to develop, mature, or progress as moral beings. As Joseph Knippenberg writes, early-modern science "undermines man's naive and prescientific belief that he is obliged to govern himself in accordance with the moral law."[17]

The nature of Kant's critique is not to reject altogether a role for modern science. Rather, it is to place limits on science that would deny its autonomy and thus make it impossible to be the grounding of true subjectivity. The *Critique of Pure Reason* is a guide to why knowledge must be limited in the interests of an overarching "faith" in the existence of free moral agency. It holds that a just epistemological "constitutional" order would regulate the use of reason—not only for its own good, that is, to prevent it from collapsing into contradiction when it overextends itself—but also in the service of morality. Once a system of recognized limits is placed on knowledge, Kant claims that even though humans inhabit a world of mechanistic natural laws that render each subject a conditioned part of the cosmos, moral autonomy is at least *possible.*[18]

Kant's novel epistemology undermines the conceits of modern science by positing what he terms a "Copernican hypothesis."[19] He claims that the relationship between the subject and the object is conceived wrongly by previous modern thinkers.[20] The subject may not passively absorb unmediated sensory impressions of an objective nature to learn nature's laws. Rather, the subject may actually determine or legislate such laws.[21] The manner in which Kant "tests" this hypothesis is a complex philosophical story, one that is beyond the modest scope of the present chapter. The most important part of this story is that a verification of this hypothesis vindicates a science or philosophical knowledge that is subordinated to the requirements of moral autonomy.

Science is limited by an ontological boundary that Kant erects between the finite, partial knowledge of which subjects are capable and the infinitely complex, supersensible "thing-in-itself" from which such claims to knowledge are derived. We cannot experience the world as it "is" because we absorb mere appearances. We make sense out of such experiences by way of concepts that reason legislates to our understanding. These concepts bracket our perceptual experiences, but they cannot be conflated, according to Kant, with the actual underlying ontological structure of nature. The finite condition of humans therefore radically limits science by preventing us from ever really knowing "things-in-themselves."[22] Paradoxically, although the subject rationally legislates its own experience of nature, we can never claim that its representations of that external reality constitute nature's underlying properties. If we do, reason only falls into contradiction. The mechanism of natural causality revealed by Newtonian science is thus not denied by Kant, but limited and placed within boundaries. Ultimately, the purpose of the Copernican hypothesis is, according to Kant, "negative."[23] Its verification and vindication prohibits the grounds of modern subjectivity from being located in an autonomous capacity to know and to transform nature, both human and nonhuman. As William James Booth writes, although "[t]he Copernican revolution places man at the centre of its account of nature [it also] limits and undermines his pretensions."[24]

The restriction of modern knowledge is intended to protect moral autonomy and thus the human subject. If human beings are fundamentally ignorant about the underlying metaphysical structure of the universe, nature cannot be shown to condition totally the individual. More precisely, our moral choices are not predetermined by our animal and embodied status. Morality, and that which makes it possible, the autonomous will, is thereby made independent from the mechanism of nature.[25] A restricted reason limits the effects of natural causality to a province that does not threaten to submerge moral agency into a system of prior determinations over which the individual has no control. However, the result of Kant's critique of knowledge is the creation of a profound dualism. Insofar as the subject is an embodied and finite creature, he is affected by the mechanism of nature. Yet because the subject is also rational, he is endowed with a moral causality that allows him to overcome and domesticate the natural world within him, that is, he is autonomous. Kant thus wishes merely to reconcile the mechanism of nature assumed by Newtonian science with the *possibility* of morality.[26] In the *Critique of Practical Reason,* he writes:

> The union of causality as freedom with causality as the mechanism of nature, the first being given through the moral law and the latter through natural law, and both as related to the same subject, man, is impossible unless man is conceived by pure consciousness as a being in itself in relation to the former, and by empirical reason as appearance in relation to the latter.[27]

The Copernican hypothesis ultimately permits Kant to posit an autonomous morality because he places morality as the unconditioned ground of subjectivity outside the realm of experience. Freedom, the basis of morality, is made initially into a regulative Idea that reason must assume but cannot demonstrate or represent.[28] Although individuals are still subject to natural causality—indeed, our very finitude and physical dependence upon nature ensure this—human freedom and dignity are preserved by the limits that Kant's critique places on knowledge.

PRACTICAL REASON: THE CRITIQUE OF SUBJECTIVITY AS POLITICAL AUTONOMY

Kant's critique of science is important because it provides him with the tools for a similar critique of modern politics. Like Newtonian science, modern politics has been fancied as an autonomous realm in which the human will is unconstrained by moral considerations. The chief exponent of a politics for its own sake is, as noted above, Machiavelli. For him, modern subjectivity is located in the ability of the individual to act with *virtù*. To act with Machiavellian virtue is to engage in political affairs with excellence, as it was for the ancients. However, unlike the ancients, political action is executed by a will that is radically separate from other beings and any external criteria. Rather, the virtue of a subject is bound up with the ability of the will to impose itself on others. It is, simultaneously, the ability to tame the greatest of obstacles to this task, the unpredictable, rebellious natural cosmos that Machiavelli symbolizes as *fortuna*. Insofar as other human beings also impede the only objective end of politics—that is, the secure domination of a self-made order—they cannot be separated easily from the *fortuna* that modern political animals are advised to seduce, and, where that fails, brutally coerce.

Machiavelli thus collapses virtue into his new vision of an autonomous politics. He does this by rendering classical Aristotelian virtue incompatible with true, "manly" political action. Modern virtue is the ability to ignore (or only pretend to obey) external standards of action located within nature or a conception of the Good.[29] By changing the meaning of virtue to express only efficiency in fulfilling the situational necessities of politics, Machiavelli seeks to remove any perceived incompatibility between virtue and politics in a peculiarly modern way. Practical action is to be based on contingent maxims that are internal to, and exhausted by, politics. The autonomy of politics is generated by a close identification of the state (*lo stato*) with an end that justifies any means for its maintenance.

Kant's practical philosophy is a critique of the autonomy of politics presupposed by early modern visions of subjectivity found not just in Machiavelli but also in Hobbes, who sees humans as fundamentally conditioned beings. The problem with such accounts of practical reasoning is that the human will is not conceived as independent from natural causality in a way that protects dignity. By rendering politics autonomous, Machiavelli subordinates the causality of the subject's will to the mechanism of nature, according to Kant. Although Machiavelli casts modern *virtù* for the sake of statecraft as a new form of civic virtue, Kant holds that practical action guided solely by instrumental rationality is ultimately an apology for self-interest based upon material or natural causes. The modern subjects who follow Machiavelli's maxims inevitably lack true substantiality because, even though they endlessly try to overcome the obstacles of nature, they act only to increase their dependence upon it because their motives are based upon *material* principles rather than—as Kant holds necessary—*formal* principles of justice. In other words, it is the nature within them, rather than the nature external to them, that individuals based on Machiavelli's vision of subjectivity are unable to transcend. An autonomous politics negates dignity because agents become the slaves of their contingent desires to dominate others; and those unable to initiate the necessary means for an effective *stato* become victims of use and abuse as there are no objective ends or formal restrictions on conduct.

In the *Critique of Pure Reason* Kant claims it necessary to reconcile the assumptions of natural mechanism with human dignity. As long as knowledge is subordinated to the requirements of morality, such an arbitration is possible. Similarly, Kant claims that modern politics and human dignity need not be incompatible.[30] To reconcile them, politics must be subordinated to the pure practical reason of morality:

> A true system of politics cannot ... take a single step without first paying tribute to morality. And although politics in itself is a difficult art, no art is required to combine it with morality. For as soon as the two come into conflict, morality can cut through the knot which politics cannot untie. ... For all politics must bend the knee before right, although politics may hope in return to arrive, however slowly, at a stage of lasting brilliance.[31]

This passage indicates that an autonomous politics cannot persist without falling into contradiction and incoherence—a claim that was also made about speculative knowledge. If politics is to acquire some coherence and achieve practical ends, it must submit to the only authentic ground of subjectivity: morality. Politics must "bend the knee" to morality even though it can achieve only a degree of "lasting brilliance" from its association with the moral realm. However, by positing morality as the ultimate location of subjectivity, Kant creates a different ontological construct to support a division of politics and morals.

KANT'S CONTRIBUTION TO MODERNITY:
THE AUTONOMY OF MORALS

Kant's critique of modernity ultimately contributes to the modern ethos because he posits another foundation for subjectivity. Morality is the only unconditioned ground upon which human dignity can be ensured. It is the only foundation that can coherently and authoritatively command and determine all of the conditioned aspects of experience. It cannot, as Kant states, be "subordinated to any other object."[32] The early-modern political thinkers who located subjectivity in other, nonmoral grounds could not but sacrifice human dignity. For if "all value were conditioned—that is, contingent—then no supreme principle can be found for reason at all."[33] The "supreme principle" at which Kant arrives is the categorical imperative, generically identified as *duty for its own sake*.[34] Without the categorical imperative there can be no dignity because "morality is the only condition under which a rational being can be an end in himself ... [and]

a law-making member in a kingdom of ends. Therefore morality, and humanity so far as it is capable of morality, is the only thing which has dignity."[35]

In order to posit morality as the autonomous ground of subjectivity, Kant states that we must, in contrast to Hobbes, eliminate from consideration all of the prior *material* causes that affect the will.[36] We must also separate the will from being informed merely by a sense of its own *efficient* causality, in contrast to Machiavelli. Lastly, the will must not act for the sake of any ends other than, as we shall see, the "kingdom of ends," the only morally objective *final* cause. This is because all particular ends pertain only to happiness, which, although substantive in Aristotelian political science, is not for Kant a sign of moral perfection. All of these causes are subject to corruption from the phenomenal world of appearances and therefore risk placing human dignity on quicksand. Thus what remains as authoritative is the *formal* cause—the cause that specifies the conditions under which willing is possible. Morality is thus initially characterized by Kant as having an entirely *a priori* or formal character. The will is to be determined only by the law that it can coherently give to itself—the law that *any* rational being could both legislate and obey unconditionally. Kant writes that the free will is "in a sphere entirely different from the empirical, and the necessity which it expresses, not being natural necessity, can consist only in the formal conditions of the possibility of law in general."[37] Morality is thus totally separated from the contingent world of lived experience. To be moral requires the subject to extirpate all heteronomous causes of the will.[38]

An autonomous morality legislates that to which the individual is not naturally inclined: to act on maxims that are objectively abstracted from all material principles of interest.[39] If politics were the autonomous ground of subjectivity, the will would operate on the basis of experience of the phenomenal world. That is, if we follow Machiavelli's advice to act on the basis of what we *actually* do, rather than what we *ought* to do, morality would be impossible.[40] Thus Kant holds that

> [i]t would be better to maintain that there are no practical laws but merely counsels for the service of our desires than to elevate merely subjective principles to the rank of practical laws, which must have an objective and not just subjective necessity and which must be known *a priori* by reason instead of by experience no matter how empirically universal.[41]

Hence, for example, the end of "success" in executing our projects is morally irrelevant. This is because the moral law "refers only to the will, irrespective of what is attained by its causality."[42] Once morality is "scrupulously separated"[43] from the contingent realm of experience, the necessary condition for true autonomy is established. The will becomes independent of the world of natural laws and the necessities of political expediency. Kant's view of subjectivity is therefore grounded only in the law that the will has by itself formulated as universal. The essence of his transformation of modern subjectivity is the claim that agency lies in the ability of finite rational beings to free themselves from natural inclination and to become self-legislating.

Yet Kant is clear to state that although morality is autonomous, it does not and cannot actually govern individuals as they empirically exist. Just as his critique of an autonomous science does not ultimately deny that individuals are subject to the forces of natural mechanism, his positing of an autonomous morality concedes that we are finite and thus inhabit an empirical world that is recalcitrant to moral virtue.[44] Indeed, it is the ontological division between our moral and phenomenal selves that enables an autonomous morality at all. This is because morality must be autonomous *from* something; for Kant it is from nature and animal instinct. An autonomous morality allows us to domesticate and transcend the world of inclination that inhabits us as we inhabit the natural cosmos. But morality can never succeed fully in enabling a transcendence of ourselves; individuals can never coincide with the perfectly "good will," and the species as a whole is nothing less than "warped wood."[45] As Kant states,

> When applied to man ... [morality] does not borrow in the slightest from acquaintance with him (in anthropology) but gives him laws *a priori* as a rational being ... for man, affected as he is by so many inclinations, is capable of the Idea of a pure practical reason, but he has not so easily the power to realize the Idea *in concreto* in his conduct of life.[46]

It is only because the subject is so divided by his rational capacity to obey laws and his natural inclinations to make an exception for his self that duty is a meaningful moral concept.[47] God and the beasts are exempt from duty because the former is not subject to instinct and the latter lack a rational will that could intervene with and subordinate inclinations.[48]

By positing an autonomous morality, Kant believes he has identified the conditions under which the nature of modern subjectivity is constitutive of human dignity, without resorting to Rousseau's seemingly blanket rejection of modern science and politics. The critical project is at root designed to provide the principles by which individuals become truly sovereign and dignified by limiting and overriding the natural causality within.[49] Thanks to morality, each individual becomes his own "Prince," dominating and mastering himself rather than others and thus creating a variant of subjectivity that recognizes the dignity of each, including herself, as an end.[50] Moral autonomy is thus for Kant the edification of modern subjectivity that earlier philosophers were content to allow to remain trapped within the "womb of nature."[51]

Nonetheless, in my view, Kant's autonomous morality does not, unhappily, overcome Machiavelli's legacy of political autonomy. From one point of view, Machiavelli does not deny the existence of morality altogether. His vision of political autonomy holds that questions of good and evil—and the standards employed to distinguish them—are ideals of *private* conscience and thus irrelevant in matters of statecraft. Kant's positing of an autonomous morality ultimately mirrors Machiavelli. In holding *either* politics *or* morals to be the exclusive foundations of modern subjectivity, both Machiavelli and Kant assert that they occupy ontologically contradictory spheres. Where these two thinkers actually differ, then, is on the question of *which* of these two radically opposed spheres—politics or morality—ought to form the determining foundation of individual subjectivity.

In reducing politics to the domination accomplished by the willing subject, Machiavelli drains it of ethical content and thereby makes morality a matter of private conscience. The radically separated individuals he depicts are concerned only with surviving the onslaught of nature or, if they possess *virtù*, with achieving a degree of permanence through their power over *fortuna*.[52] Similarly, by restricting ethics to a realm of pure practical reason and duty for its own sake, Kant strips politics of any *inherent* connection to morality. This is because an autonomous morality must be located outside the phenomenal realm of human interests and conditioned ends that constitute politics. Kant locates individual subjectivity on an ontologically higher plane than the ambiguous world of politics. Politics can be touched by, but never be truly constitutive of, ethical life. In thus elevating morality beyond the realm of experience, Kant reinforces Machiavelli's alienation of politics from morality because, in the end, he finds it doubtful "whether any genuine virtue is actually to be encountered in the world."[53] Because the motives involved in politics are invariably mixed and corrupted with the particularity and contingency of interests, morality for Kant seems to also become a matter of private conscience.

Although Kant reproduces Machiavelli's chasm between politics and morals, he actually wishes to bring them together again through the realization of justice. The most important consequence of Kant's reaction to precritical philosophy is the ontological chasm he opens between the moral autonomy of subjects and the political world that is itself devoid of moral content. This dualism creates the necessity of a project to reform politics. This project is one of transforming relations among individuals to reflect, but at the same time not sacrifice, their sacred moral autonomy. Alternatively stated, Kant holds that the goal of politics is to subordinate its practice—to the largest and widest possible extent—to the same pattern or logic of universal, formal principles that is found in morality.

CONCLUSION

This necessarily condensed account of the foundations of Kant's political philosophy shall serve as a kind of foundation for the remainder of this book. The main elements of Kant's political philosophy emerge from his unique response to early-modern depictions of individual subjectivity. Although he accepts the notion that the individual is radically distinct from the natural cosmos, he contests the location of subjectivity in the capacity to *know* the world and—more crucially—to *will* upon maxims of political expediency. Kant proposes an alternative ground of subjectivity that he claims is the only authentic ground of freedom from nature, and our inherent dignity: an *autonomous morality*. The Kantian political project is, however, fraught with ambiguity. The source of this ambiguity is his own ontological separation of morals and politics that results from his peculiar depiction of human subjectivity. The nature of this ambiguity is that the core of Kant's critical system, the "architectonic" symbol of freedom that forms his vision of justice, is divided. Kant's philosophy is divided by his concept of freedom into two ontological spheres: the moral and the political.

CHAPTER 2

THE ETHICO-POLITICAL AMBIGUITY OF KANTIAN FREEDOM

The concept of freedom … is the keystone of the whole architecture of the system of pure reason and even of speculative reason.

—Kant[1]

Human freedom is at the core of Kant's thought. We cannot adequately explain any particular aspect of his legacy without ultimately viewing it in relation to this concept—what Kant claims is the "keystone" of his critical philosophy. The present chapter reconstructs and interprets the central place of freedom in shaping Kant's theory of justice and thereby develops a conceptual framework. This framework will explain the place of sovereignty in Kant's vision of justice. It is because freedom is the ground, and therefore the justification, for Kant's vision of political reform that this mode of analysis is justified.

Kant's concept of freedom is affected deeply by the ontological division of morals and politics that has been identified. The gulf between morals and politics is ostensibly reconciled by the supremacy of the categorical imperative. However, individuals remain ever divided by a radical difference between the noumenal world of pure morality and the phenomenal world in which politics occurs. For this reason, Kant's conception of justice is shaped by two distinct types of freedom, the "internal" and the "external." The distinction that Kant makes between these two sides of individual freedom constitutes his most profound statement on the relationship between an autonomous morality and political practice. By reconstructing Kant's arguments in favor of their distinction, we see the dynamics behind his theory of justice: The pure practical reason of morality (inner freedom) *informs*—and thereby subordinates—the structure of outer freedom and the political reality with which it is associated.

Nonetheless, this conceptual framework reveals that there is profound ethico-political ambivalence within this internal/external division. Kant's distinction between the two sides of freedom does not merely indicate that morality must subordinate and determine the political world. The differentiation is also predicated upon a great limitation on the extent to which politics *can* (and therefore *ought*) to be subordinated to morality. In actuality, Kant argues that the morality of internal freedom only legislates the basic universal *form* of external freedom and politics. Morality cannot, however, legitimately legislate the *ends* that are essential to the categorical imperative of internal freedom into the external realm of just political relations among individuals. But I show that this relationship between the two sides of Kantian freedom produces ambiguity, for it is not at all clear that moral ends can possibly be, or ought to be, completely abstracted from politics in the manner that Kant sometimes seems to suggest. Indeed, there is evidence from Kant's own texts that he is uncertain about the stricture against moral ends as the incentive for political practice and reform. I claim that Kant's multifarious concept of freedom is the key to explaining the shape of his theory of justice generally. As will be shown, the ambiguities produced by his peculiar division of freedom account for the paradoxical stance he adopts on state sovereignty and the vision of international reform that he propounds.

There are three sections in this chapter. In the first, I situate Kant's reputation as a political philosopher within differing contemporary depictions of his view of the nature of freedom. Although there have been attempts to characterize him as a proponent of either "positive" or "negative" freedom alone, Kant's theory of justice is far more complicated than the terms of this distinction (famously posited by Isaiah Berlin). The second section outlines a framework to explain why justice takes the form that it does in Kant's thought. In separating internal from external freedom, Kant articulates his view of the proper relationship between morality and politics and the fundamental logic of all political reform. The realization of justice is how politics is to be subordinated to, and informed by, the same formal principles found in morality. The third section shows the limits and ambiguities of the Kantian vision of reform in relation to his conception of justice. This is done by demonstrating how the basic autonomy of morals that is a foundation of his philosophy dictates that politics be concerned primarily with formal principles of justice alone, and then only indirectly with the realization of moral purposes.

INTERPRETING FREEDOM IN KANT'S LEGACY

Isaiah Berlin's essay "Two Concepts of Liberty" is an important reference point for any discussion of freedom in modern political thought. There are few clearer expressions of the divisions and dilemmas inherent in the concept than the distinction Berlin makes between negative and positive freedom. The former pertains to the absence of external impediments and noninterference with the subject; the latter concerns the ideals of self-mastery and self-determination.[2] Nonetheless, one difficulty with this distinction is that it is sometimes held to be of transhistorical significance, illuminating various "doctrines" of liberty from the ancient Greeks to the present.[3]

Berlin's formulation of the distinction between negative and positive freedoms has a certain applicability to Kant. However, as my conceptual framework will show, it can lead to a very partial view of his theory of justice. This is because although Kant, too, uses the vocabulary of the negative and the positive to describe certain dimensions of his concept of freedom, he denies (misleadingly, as will become apparent) any *political* importance to this distinction. For Kant locates such a distinction solely within the individual's internal, moral subjectivity, which is separated from the world of politics. We cannot therefore simply associate Berlin's positive liberty with Kant's internal (moral) freedom and negative liberty with what Kant calls external (political) freedom. Berlin assumes that negative and positive freedom are ultimately and necessarily in "direct conflict" with each other.[4] This contrasts greatly with Kant's presentation of these terms; indeed, his theory of justice is structured upon the ostensible compatibility of the positive and the negative dimensions of freedom as he defines them. Negative and positive freedoms are compatible because they are rooted within a more significant dichotomy that Kant makes between the internal and external sides of freedom. The ensuing analysis will show that Kant's own ambiguity and ambivalence on the ethico-political meaning of freedom emanates from the division between internal and external freedom.

It is no small wonder that there is a great deal of disagreement over how to characterize Kant's political thought. This is especially true when Berlin's assumptions shape the debate. Berlin refers to Kant as the paradigmatic example of a philosopher of positive freedom, citing as evidence the categorical imperative and the moral autonomy it presupposes. In this way Kant is a foil for Berlin to criticize the positive conception of freedom as a potentially despotic deviation from the original, negative essence of liberty in modern liberalism.[5] Elie Kedourie amplifies and extends Berlin's claims, linking Kant's ideal of individual self-determination to the historical development of the chauvinistic politics of nationalism.[6] However, both authors minimize the existence of another dimension of freedom in Kant's texts, one that is much closer to—but by no means coeval with— the negative freedom that they seem to prefer in classical liberalism.[7] The difficulty with the Berlin and Kedourie depictions of Kant's politics is their reliance upon a caricature of Kant's morality. This problem is a consequence of their apparent ignorance of his larger theory of justice that is designed to establish the proper relationship between morality and politics.

To scholars who have paid closer attention to Kant's texts, Berlin's and Kedourie's statements are bizarre and misleading. Some have thus sought to counter such misrepresentations, and, in so doing, may have gone too far in the other direction. For example, Howard Williams demonstrates the lack of evidence for the Berlin and Kedourie positions,[8] and argues that Kant's politics are actually premised on a "negative concept of freedom."[9] Similarly, Otfried Höffe denies altogether the view that Kant's conception of political liberty is oriented exclusively by the moral principle of "positive" autonomy (found in the *Groundwork of the Metaphysic of Morals* or the *Critique of Practical Reason*).[10] The Williams and Höffe positions rest correctly on the fact that Kant, in his theory of justice in the *Metaphysics of Morals,* explicitly denies that his moral principle of autonomy can or ought to constitute directly the political relations among individuals in civil society, or, as we shall see, among states in international society.

Although Williams and Höffe are correct to insist that Kant's theory of justice is not simply the application of the moral categorical imperative to politics, they perhaps "overreact" to the misreading found in Berlin and Kedourie. This is because they take Kant's own insistence upon the purely formal structure of justice as a set of principles that do not contain moral ends or purposes. There is, however, profound ambiguity within Kant's view of justice because it is unclear whether the relationship between morals and politics upon which it rests is ultimately, purely formal. Williams's and Höffe's depiction of Kant's concept of political freedom begins to resemble too greatly the classical heritage of mere negative liberty, rather than the profound challenge it is to the underlying ontological and moral assumptions of earlier liberalism.

Interpreting the nature of Kant's view of freedom leads to an explanation of justice and the reform of state and international politics it supports. Although justice is constituted by the foundational dualism within Kant's philosophy of freedom, it is also made ambiguous as a consequence. The dichotomy between the internal (moral) and external (legal-political) spheres and the tension between them is most relevant in this context.[11] As a consequence of this division, the nature of Kant's connection with modern liberalism is not straightforward. As Charles Taylor notes, Kant's writings display a strong "libertarian" concern for noninterference with the individual[12] *and* a vision of political society as a positive ideal—as something that "integrates the free subject into the community of men."[13] In light of the above interpretive and substantive points, the conceptual framework outlined below takes the division between the internal and the external sides of freedom as a basis to explain the problems with Kant's view of justice as a motivation for political reform.

The Moral Legislation of Politics

The division that Kant makes between internal and external freedom is essential to his theory of justice and stakes out the basic conditions of Kantian political reform. Yet this distinction also greatly complicates the nature of these things. The distinction constitutes his thought on justice because it is the principal means by which he explains how an autonomous morality gradually informs and subordinates politics. However, the distinction also complicates this Kantian project of reforming the political world in line with universal moral precepts because, by separating the internal from the external sides of freedom, he also places strict *limitations* on the extent to which morality can and ought to inform the political world. The ensuing reconstruction of Kant's distinction between the internal and external clarifies Kant's texts with a framework that shows why justice—as a motive for political reform—leads to conflicting demands on sovereign states in the process of international change.

Prior to the *Metaphysics of Morals,* Kant did not give a definitive and systematic division to freedom between a moral (noumenal) realm and a political (phenomenal) realm, each of which is located separately inside and outside of the individual.[14] Such a division, however, is anticipated in the *Critique of Practical Reason* in passages such as this:

> Empirical grounds of decision are not fit for any *external* legislation, and they are just as little suited to an *internal,* for each man makes his own subject the foundation for his inclination, and in each person it is now one and now another inclination which has preponderance.[15]

What is already evident here is Kant's view that the two sides of freedom have one overriding similarity: They are both based on *formal* principles, not on *ends* or material incentives. It is only seven years later, in the *Metaphysics of Morals,* that Kant explicitly grounds his theory of justice in relation to a division between internal and external freedom and, more crucially, a *priority* of formal over material principles. This work is structured by a separation between a "Doctrine of Right" (the conditions of external freedom) and a "Doctrine of Virtue" (internal freedom). As Kant writes,

> This distinction, on which the main division of the doctrine of morals as a whole also rests, is based on this: that the concept of *freedom*, which is common to both, makes it necessary to divide duties into duties which are of *outer freedom* and duties of *inner freedom*, only the latter of which are ethical.[16]

However, even though this division in the *Metaphysics of Morals* is his mature and final statement on freedom, we cannot ignore his previous declarations on this concept in the *Groundwork* and the *Critiques*. The reconstruction that follows supports my claim that the morality of internal freedom is intended to *subordinate* politics insofar as it provides it with a *formal* structure. Internal freedom *informs* external freedom; but this attempted subordination is incomplete and ultimately impossible: It produces ambiguity at the heart of Kant's theory of justice and the view of political reform it supports (Table 2.1).

Table 2.1   The Two Sides of Freedom in Kant's Account of Justice

Side	Negative (*Willkür*)	Positive (*Wille*)	MOTIVE to ACT
Internal Freedom MORALITY	Independence from nature or material causes (i.e., inclinations)	Autonomy: obedience to the objective laws that one's reason produces	Incentive is internal and autonomous: duty or reverence for the moral law
↓	↓	↓	↓

KANT'S AIM: The *moral* realm subordinates and gives *form* to the *political* realm without losing its autonomous status.

↓	↓	↓	↓
External Freedom LEGALITY (POLITICS)	Justice (*Recht*): the equal limitation of outer freedom of choice of subjects	Original Contract (Idea): common subordination to a republican order of laws to which one consents	Incentive is external and heteronomous: obligation an impure mixture of coercion, self-interest, and, increasingly, duty

(The necessity of a sovereign)

Internal Freedom: Negative and Positive

Internal freedom becomes "internal" only when Kant places the subject into a phenomenal world of other wills "external" to it. That is, it is only once he turns his attention to the more concrete and conditioned world of politics and the external relations among individuals that the word "internal" becomes pertinent. Internal freedom is, strictly speaking, *apolitical* because its pure moral autonomy depends upon its being divorced from experience.[17] It is that part of humans that is noumena, and thus the incentive to act is purely from duty and from no other heterogeneous or material factors.

In his ethical writings Kant divides the inner (moral) side of freedom into the negative (Willkür) and positive (Wille).[18] In the *Critique of Practical Reason,* for example, he writes the following:

> The sole principle of morality consists in independence from all material of the law (i.e., a desired object) and in the accompanying determination of choice by the mere form of giving universal law which a maxim must be capable of having. That independence, however, is freedom in the negative sense, while this intrinsic legislation of pure and thus practical reason is freedom in the positive sense.[19]

Negative freedom refers here to an important characteristic feature of Kant's view of subjectivity, viz., the will overcoming nature and the material impulses and desires that the latter causes. By contrast, positive freedom is the will determining itself through self-legislation. Kant holds these two aspects of freedom to be necessarily compatible and to "reciprocally imply each other."[20] Negative freedom precedes and enables positive freedom. Thus, to strive toward the ideal of the "good will" that is autonomous and self-legislating, the individual must first make fundamental *choices* about which maxims to follow, and such choice is essentially a negative task of purging material causes.[21] The negative and positive distinction is also important because, as will become apparent below, these two dimensions have correlates in the realm of external freedom, where Kant uses the *Wille* and *Willkür* terminology again.[22]

To understand the meaning of positive, inner freedom, it is necessary to consider the categorical imperative. This moral law contains several ambiguities, most of which are beyond the scope of this analysis. The ambiguities stem from the different, related formulations that Kant gives to this imperative. Although Bernard Carnois claims that there are five distinct representations of the moral law by Kant,[23] I am concerned only with the three most prominent in the *Groundwork of the Metaphysic of Morals:* (i) autonomy; (ii) universality; and (iii) the humanity principle.

Whereas the first two principles give inner freedom (or morality) a formal character, the humanity principle goes beyond formalism by imposing *ends* upon individual subjects.

The *autonomy* of the will is the supreme condition of, and logically prior to, the other formulations of the categorical imperative.[24] Kant states that it is "the Idea *of the will of every rational being as a will which makes universal law.*"[25] Without autonomy, morality is impossible. For, unlike negative freedom (*Willkür*), autonomy (*Wille*) is not merely a choice among many different possibilities via the rejection of the heteronomous grounds of action. Autonomy means that only *one* choice can be considered moral: that which reason legislates as objectively necessary. The ideal of autonomy as positive freedom has, as will be shown below, a rough correlate in external freedom (or the political world): It is Kant's concept of active citizens in a republic built upon the idea of an "original contract." However, the distinguishing feature of internal autonomy is that its motives are—unlike in the external, political world—purely self-legislated. The only incentive for action under the autonomy formula is duty: "[T]he necessity for me to act out of *pure reverence* for the law is what constitutes duty, to which every other motive must give way because it is the condition of the good will *in itself*, whose value is above all else."[26]

The categorical imperative is renowned for its insistence on *universality*. Kant intends to provide a formal explanation of how the will abstracts from its choice everything that is heteronomous and negates it. As he writes in the *Critique of Practical Reason,* "Only a formal law, that is, one which prescribes to reason nothing more than the form of its universal legislation as the supreme condition of maxims, can be *a priori* a determining ground of practical reason."[27] In the *Groundwork* he states this formal requirement as follows: "I ought never to act except in such a way *that I can also will that my maxim should become a universal law.*"[28] As I shall claim below, this dimension of internal freedom provides the basic *form* for external freedom and the kind of political justice it requires.

Hegel complains that Kant's morality is only formal and does not therefore prescribe concrete duties or substantive ends.[29] Internal freedom appears to be entirely indeterminate and empty because, in removing everything concrete, the autonomous will does not relate to the content of duties. This would be simply true were it not for the third formulation of the categorical imperative: The moral law also gives internal freedom content by prescribing an unconditioned and objective end, the end Kant calls "humanity."[30] The *humanity* principle states that the person is an objective end and must be treated only as an end *per se* and never as mere means: "Now morality is the only condition under which a rational being can be an end in himself; for only through this is it possible to be a law-making member of a kingdom of ends. Therefore morality, and humanity so far as it is capable of morality, is the only thing which has dignity."[31] It is because the human is the only creature that can set *ends* undetermined by the natural, phenomenal world and its material causes that he or she is capable of morality. Kant claims that it is because of this dignified position in the cosmos that each individual must be recognized as an objective end imposing duties on all to legislate humanity as an end that cannot be subordinated to any instrumental purposes. The existence of objective ends legislating morality means that Kant's ethics are not merely formal, but substantive too.[32] This substantive end, once recognized, necessarily engenders a *material* cause of the will insofar as it requires us to recognize others as ends and to treat them accordingly. Nonetheless, the extent to which this material end informs Kant's view of justice and thereby motivates political reform is ambiguous. This ambiguity affects the character of the international reform project he prescribes.

External Freedom and Justice

As Leslie Arthur Mulholland writes, the basis of Kant's account of ethics, "including political and social ethics," is "the contention that consciousness of the moral law must precede any understanding of freedom and rights."[33] Although this kind of priority within Kant's vision of the moral sphere over the political is true, it is also crucial to realize that morals and politics are, by nature, ontologically alienated. By articulating a theory of justice, however, Kant attempts to provide the principles by which to reconcile these two spheres while maintaining the sovereignty of morality over the political—the moral law provides the form, but not the substantive content, of justice. Thus justice and the rights and duties that constitute it are derived from the formal structure of the moral reasoning found in internal freedom.

It is my argument that in Kant's theory of justice, internal freedom and morality is intended only to *inform* and to therefore *subordinate* external freedom and politics. This Kantian doctrine points to a reform project of the political world in line with universal moral principles. However, there are crucial limits that are placed on this reform project that are inherent within, and supported by, Kant's distinction of the internal and external sides of freedom. This reconstruction of Kant's distinction between internal and external freedom reveals how and why morality ideally subordinates politics and provides the critical tools for rational political reform. Kant claims that the questions of justice that constitute external freedom are animated by the same general principles that characterize morality.[34] As we shall see, this means that morality subordinates nature insofar as the contingent and lawless relations among individuals are reformed on the basis of the universal and lawful principles comprised by morality. To see why and how politics must submit to the *formal* principles of morality, we must examine first how the structure of external freedom is imbued with the same *a priori* formal structure that characterizes the categorical imperative.

We already know from the previous chapter why politics must submit to morality. Politics is the realm of natural inclinations and phenomenal appearances; and therefore the standards that might possibly constitute and give shape to its boundaries, and our action within those parameters, cannot be taken from politics. Politics cannot be (entirely) sovereign for Kant. This is because the political world is *essentially* one of contingent, not formal-universal, causes; that is, within the mechanism of nature and the political relations that emerge from it, there is no inherent respect for humanity. Hence Kant writes that politics must at the very least "pay tribute" to morality by adhering to the formal universality of moral principles.[35] The formal causality found in morality must be made to precede all material causes in our conception of politics, that is, politics must be conceived primarily *a priori* rather than in Machiavelli's terms of how things are actually done. As Kant writes in "Perpetual Peace,"

> To ensure that practical philosophy is at one with itself, it is first necessary to resolve the question of whether, in problems of practical reason, we should begin from its material principle, that is, its end (as an object of the will), or from its formal principle [...]. The latter principle must undoubtedly take precedence.[36]

Elsewhere he writes: "Thus it is based on *a priori* principles, for experience cannot provide knowledge of what is right, that there is a *theory* of political rights to which practice must conform before it can be valid."[37] It is because *form* takes priority over *matter* that morality subordinates politics.[38] Justice is thus an attempt by Kant to reconcile morality and politics in a way that enshrines and ensures the autonomy of the former and—equally important—provides a basis for the reform of the latter. Indeed, it is the autonomy of morals that makes inner freedom the appropriate model for external freedom, a distinction that contains the presumed need for and essential direction of reform.

However, Kant's theory of justice is made complex and ambiguous because, as we shall see below, it is not simply a moralization of politics. The autonomy of morals does not only legislate the formal requirements

THE ETHICO-POLITICAL AMBIGUITY OF KANTIAN FREEDOM

of just politics—it also demands strict limitations upon the influence of moral ends within the political world. That is, constitutional limits are imposed on the project of rationally reforming politics in line with morality. Hence, there exist crucial differences according to Kant between principles of morality and principles of politics, even though the former ought to supply the essential form of the latter.

The application of the formal principles of morality to politics through *a priori* principles results in two related dimensions of Kant's concept of external freedom. The first is a form of negative freedom that he calls Right (*Recht*). The second aspect is a positive freedom enabled by Right that he calls the Idea of an "original contract." These two related dimensions of external freedom receive their shape from the two correlate dimensions of inner freedom, that is, negative (*Willkür*) and positive (*Wille*). The next chapter demonstrates why Kant's doctrine of state sovereignty—as an instrument of political justice—receives its most explicit justification from these aspects of outer liberty.

Kant's account of external freedom relies on a contrast with lawlessness or anarchy.[39] Liberty under anarchic conditions is unstable, insecure, and radically contingent because we are subject to violence and unsanctioned coercion upon our will by others. As a consequence, anarchy completely negates the very possibility of the *ends* that each individual can set. Thus Kant's justification for reforming politics by transcending the state of nature is purely *a priori* and does not lie in any conceivable calculation of interest and self-interest. The necessity to "domesticate" man's phenomenal side is not grounded upon empirical, but rather transcendental, considerations. As Allen D. Rosen notes, the requirement of justice has a fundamental *structural* rationale: "[I]n the event of a dispute between individuals about their respective rights, no impartial system of adjudication could ensure non-arbitrary settlement."[40]

External freedom is interrelated, then, with justice or Right (*Recht*) and the conditions that are necessarily opposed to the state of nature: a sovereign state, the subject of the next chapter. Here Kant uses the analogue of *Willkür* found in internal freedom to give shape to its phenomenal, political realization. Right has the negative connotation of independence from the constraints imposed by other wills.[41] This independence is logically inconceivable in the state of nature. In order to secure a condition of Right, Kant posits a "universal law of justice" that stipulates a *limit* upon each individual's external freedom in order to ensure a basic compatibility of each will's external freedom. As Rosen notes, this is an "externalized" version of the formal universality principle of the categorical imperative.[42] As Kant states, "[a]ny action is right if it can coexist with everyone's freedom in accordance with a universal law."[43] More generally, "Right is … the sum of conditions under which the choice of one can be united with the [negative] choice of another in accordance with a universal law of freedom."[44] The external freedom of Right, then, is moral insofar as it imposes categorical duties that are abstracted from any material ends. However, it is political because it concerns only external relations among individuals, and how their actions affect each other.[45]

Kant's concept of external freedom is not, however, merely negative liberty. This is because the freedom of Right described above is a crucial prerequisite for what he calls the Idea of an original contract.[46] It is this aspect of Kant's concept of freedom that legislates most explicitly a project for the continual reform of state sovereignty, as will be discussed in the next chapter. The Idea that political practice must gradually approximate is that of a republican constitution. This is because only this particular arrangement of external freedom realizes concretely moral autonomy in the political world. The Idea is not merely based upon Right, but also functions to secure external relations in a way that is wholly consistent with our unique human capacity to set *ends*. Here Kant pays homage to Rousseau by stating that it is only the common subordination of each individual to a system of laws to which he has freely consented that is truly legitimate.[47] This notion of self-legislation is different from the mere instrumentality of quitting the state of nature. As Kant writes,

> And one cannot say: the human being in a state [that approximates the Idea] has sacrificed a *part* of his innate outer freedom for the sake of an end, but rather, he has relinquished entirely his wild, lawless freedom in order to find his freedom as such undiminished, in a dependence upon laws, that is, in a rightful condition, since this dependence arises from his own law-giving will.[48]

The Idea of an original contract thus suggests that external freedom also requires the content of autonomy that animates the categorical imperative.[49] It is for this reason that Taylor claims Kant's republicanism "is also constitutive of moral agency."[50] Nonetheless, I now argue for the importance of profound limits imposed on the moral impact upon politics that Kant's concept of freedom reveals.

THE LIMITATIONS OF MORAL FREEDOM AND KANT'S AMBIGUITY

In this section my approach shifts from being primarily exegetical because I consider the ambiguities that are produced by Kant's dualistic understanding of freedom and ask why they arise. By examining the distinction

Kant makes between internal and external freedom I have shown *how*, through the idea of justice, morality subordinates and thereby "domesticates" politics. Nonetheless, the distinction between internal and external freedom in the *Metaphysics of Morals* is not merely about moral legislation—it is equally about the restriction of the moral sphere in politics. For Kant also limits and circumscribes the determining influence of morality on politics. He describes these limits by positing two related distinctions. He first claims a difference between *morality* and *legality*, terms that are based upon the radically different types of incentives that underlie internal and external obligations. He then speaks about the difference between *form* and *ends*, which arises when the material and teleological purposes of the categorical imperative—inherent in the humanity principle—are removed from the scope of external freedom.

The distinction between *morality* and *legality* is necessary for Kant given his view of the nature of subjectivity. To be considered moral, an action must be performed *for the sake of duty* alone; the incentive to act must be absolutely unconditioned. Even though the *Critique of Practical Reason* only anticipates the full division between internal and external freedom, in it Kant notes the importance of the two different kinds of motive that inspire them:

> What is essential in the moral worth of actions is that the moral law should directly determine the will. If the determination of the will occurs in accordance with the moral law but only by means of a feeling of any kind whatsoever, which must be presupposed in order that the law may become the determining ground of the will, and if the action does not occur for the sake of the law, it has legality but not morality.[51]

In the *Metaphysics of Morals* he states that morals (virtue) and politics (legality) are "distinguished not so much by their different duties as by the difference in their lawgiving. ... "[52] Moral lawgiving has the inner incentive of duty alone, but legal lawgiving can at best only coincide with the act prescribed by morality because its incentive is conditioned, and therefore, ultimately, "pathological."[53] When the heteronomous incentives of "inclinations and aversions" that emanate from relations in civil society and the laws of the state inspire action, it is only legality that forms the basis of obligation. Kant is concerned here that the mere performance of duties prescribed by external relations will be falsely portrayed as having an inherently moral quality: "[W]hen one's aim is not to teach virtue but only to set forth what is *right*, one may not and should not represent that law of right as itself the incentive to action."[54] The danger with the illusion that the state or any other worldly authority must teach virtue is that it will lead to the imposition of contingent and materially based ends upon individuals. As Höffe states, "Kant rejects the position that the law and the state should promote the citizen's morality (virtue). Such moralizing tends toward totalitarianism."[55] Thus the distinction between morality and legality is aimed at limiting the extent to which morality can legitimately legislate external relations in a phenomenal world. In other words, it is a distinction that is crucial for the possibility of political autonomy.

The distinction between legality and morality actually corresponds to and emanates from the more fundamental division in Kant's thought between *formal* and *material* causes. Kant apparently abstracts or purges all ends and purposes from justice. As noted above, the categorical imperative has both a formal dimension of pure universality and a teleological and substantive humanity principle that produces an internal obligation to act as a member of the "kingdom of ends." In defining Right, Kant initially allows only the formal cause of universality to determine the shape of external freedom; all legislated moral ends must be abstracted. Therefore, Right concerns only the *form* of the relations of individuals in a shared external world, not their internal wishes, desires, or ends (no matter how potentially "moral" such goals might be).[56] This is contrasted sharply with morality. So much is evident when Kant introduces his explicitly apolitical "Doctrine of Virtue," the second part of the *Metaphysics of Morals*:

> The doctrine of right dealt only with the *formal* condition of outer freedom (the consistency of outer freedom with itself if its maxim were made universal law), that is, with right. But ethics goes beyond this and provides a *matter* (an object of free choice), an end of pure reason which it represents as an end that is also objectively necessary, that is, an end that, as far as human beings are concerned, it is a duty to have. For since the sensible inclinations of human beings tempt them to ends (the matter of choice) that can be contrary to duty, lawgiving reason can in turn check their influence only by a moral end set up against the ends of inclination, an end that must therefore be given *a priori*, independently of inclinations.[57]

Kant wishes here to forestall any "incursion into ethics" by politically expedient goals.[58] For all political ends can ultimately be traced back to the antecedent prior causes that are rooted in nonformal aims of interest and self-interest.[59] Kant's modification of his moral theory to include a distinction between internal and external freedom results from his view that the obligations imposed by the categorical imperative could not simply be created or introduced into the phenomenal world of political reality, at least not without being compromised severely. This is why, as Pogge notes, the categorical imperative, which dominated the discussions in the

Groundwork and second *Critique,* does not play a central role in the "Doctrine of Right."[60] The distinction thus clarifies Kant's philosophy because it answers the question of "the appropriate extent of morally mandated coercion: Force may (and should) be used for justice only. Persons should be coerced exactly insofar as it is necessary to meet reason's demand for the compatibility of our domains of external freedom."[61] However, this solution is not entirely unambiguous in its results. It has opened up controversy over how we interpret and apply Kantian justice to politics.

In truth, Kant does not actually wish to limit the extent to which politics is reformed on the basis of moral principles; he wants to increase it. However, this interpretation of his dualistic concept of freedom reveals something important about his political philosophy in general. The two above distinctions actually serve to limit and restrict the legislative force of morality within the political world. This restriction is based on Kant's firm conviction that although all proper political reform is based upon universal principles derived from morality, all such reform projects are doomed at best—and dangerous at worst—unless the essential *autonomy of morality* is preserved. In other words, the ultimate location of human subjectivity must be kept firmly in the realm of pure practical reason; and politics must always be kept in a subordinated realm of experience. This deeper ontological vision is stated in the *Critique of Practical Reason* as follows: "[R]espect for the [moral] law is not the drive to morality: it is morality itself ... by rejecting all the rival claims of self-love, [that] gives authority and absolute sovereignty to the law."[62]

However, the key here is that this supreme justification produces ambiguity and paradox at the heart of Kant's political philosophy. The goal of subordinating politics to morality is complicated by the restrictions and legislative limits inherent in the distinction between internal and external freedom. On the one hand, the absolute sovereignty of the moral realm appears to deny that *any* activity or institution in the political sphere can contribute to individual autonomy. As Rosen notes, "The complete absence of external freedom would not diminish positive or negative [i.e., inner] freedom in the slightest .... The justification of external freedom cannot, consequently, be derived from the moral necessity of inner freedom."[63] Politics cannot, it would seem, be used simply as an instrument for realizing the "kingdom of ends" on earth.

But this view of Kant cannot be sustained. Ambiguity creeps into Kant's thought because there are clear instances where his justification of society and external freedom logically entails the moral ends of inner freedom. The politics of external freedom cannot be ends in themselves for Kant; consistent and universal external liberty must receive its value from what it secures for the ultimate ground of our dignity: our moral autonomy. Hence politics would seem to have an implicit moral purpose or end, and the sovereign state is a crucial agent in moral development.

In the *Critique of Practical Reason* Kant stresses that although morality cannot be enforced, the legal framework of the state provides a much needed push-start toward individual moral realization:

> Certainly it cannot be denied that in order to bring an as yet uneducated or a degraded mind into the path of the morally good, some preparatory guidance is needed to attract it by a view to its own advantage or to frighten it by fear of harm. As soon as this machinery, these leading strings, have had some effect, the pure moral motive must be brought to mind.[64]

Politics has a moral function, therefore, in providing the mechanism by which a "master" or sovereign breaks the "self-will" of each individual and forces him or her "to obey a universally valid will under which everyone can be free."[65] As Patrick Riley states, Kant's thrust here is that the phenomenal world of (just) politics and universal laws creates "a kind of environment or context for good will by bracketing out occasions of political sin (such as others' domination) that might tempt (though never determine) people to act wrongly."[66] Although the machinations of the sovereign state can never be moral in themselves, they can serve indirectly certain moral ends by transcending the state of nature. By creating consistent domains of external liberty for individuals, and enforcing such domains from unlawful coercion, the moral goal of autonomy is an ambiguous goal of political reform for Kant. Moreover, as we shall see in the next chapter, the justification of the sovereign state is bound up with this relationship between morals and politics within Kantian justice.

The existence of injustice requires political reform. Nonetheless, the nature of this reform is made problematic by the peculiar nature of Kant's justice. Even if we accept that politics has a "moral" function by providing a stable context outside of the state of nature, the entirely *formal* structure of equal domains of external freedom does not exhaust his vision of politics. There may indeed be moral ends in addition to basic independence from lawlessness that can be facilitated through political reform. That is, if anarchy is an impediment to moral autonomy that can be overcome by justice, politics may have a role in producing more profound moral goals. Is politics merely *formal* as he states over and over again, or is there also a *material* principle in Kant's thought that promotes the humanity principle of treating each individual as an end? The ideal of the "kingdom of ends" may conceivably be facilitated through politics. It is generally agreed that the ideals of the individual good will and the kingdom of ends have *some* bearing on the external and phenomenal world of politics for Kant.

The question is, however, do these moral principles act as mere *regulative* ideals or is there a *material* basis for their realization too? Here there is mixed evidence in Kant's own texts that allow for two divergent interpretations, one "conservative" and the other "radical."

The conservative answer to this question—both interpretively and politically—is that the kingdom of ends is merely regulative and is therefore only in the service of experience. Although all ends must be abstracted from Right, Kant suggests frequently that the systematic harmony of purposes that motivates our inner freedom serves only as a symbolic device organizing external relations.[67] In this case, "the *idea* of an ethical commonwealth generated by the good will serves as a kind of utopia that earthly politics can legally approximate through peacefulness, both internal and international."[68] But in such a reading, the mere symbolic application of the good will and the kingdom of ends to politics is limited. Moral ends are permanently and ontologically alienated from the political world; their practical legislation onto reality must always be *formal.*[69]

A much more radical response to this ambiguity emerges if we follow Pogge, for example, and focus on Kant's concept of progressive enlightenment.[70] Pogge suggests that enlightenment means that the material purpose or end of the categorical imperative is projected into politics as well. And there is evidence, both in terms of the texts and of logical implication, that Kant considered his politics to have this material dimension too, although it occupies a secondary position relative to the formal cause. This possibility emerges if we consider that Kant's concept of history serves to bridge the sharp chasms between nature and moral freedom that he first posits. The material principle of enlightenment is, most generally, that reason is promoted and advanced in the political world. As Pogge writes:

> Kant introduces the material aspect of pure practical reason in his theory of *justice.* This engenders his *material* principle of justice which demands (roughly) the thriving of reason and the promotion of its development in the species and in each particular person. This principle, as opposed to the formal one, is teleological ... [and gives] politics some definite long-term goals.[71]

This material principle hence gives political reform a much more profound moral incentive that appeared to be initially restricted or disallowed by the terms of Kant's distinction between inner and outer freedom. However, if the formal grounding of political freedom and justice is not jeopardized by the introduction of material causes into the project of reforming reality, Kant does not see a problem with such incentives. As the

next chapter demonstrates, the moral incentive of a kingdom of ends justifies political action, reform, and institutional change under the strict
condition that the formal mechanisms guaranteed by the sovereign are
not destroyed by revolutionary, lawless upheaval. For reform and change
are part of a slow process:

> All man's talents are now gradually developed, his taste cultivated, and by a
> continual process of enlightenment, a beginning is made towards establish-
> ing a way of thinking that can with time transform the primitive natural
> capacity for moral discrimination into definite practical principles; and
> thus a *pathologically* enforced social union is transformed into a *moral
> whole.*[72]

Thus the (material) purposes of politics emerge in an ambiguous fashion
in Kant's thought. The aim is to condition humans to act in such a way
that a kingdom of ends is possible; but this conditioning cannot teach
virtue directly—the sovereign can provide only the underlying conditions
in which the moral choice of each to become a member of such a kingdom is enabled. As William A. Galston states, "[I]t is here that the inner
tension of his politico-moral thought becomes most manifest.... Kant's
teleological doctrine of human perfection thus exerts an irresistible
pressure on the limits of the neutral state."[73]

CONCLUSION

Kant's view of justice is constituted by a fundamental distinction between
internal and external freedom. This chapter employed a conceptual
framework to interpret the relationship of these two sides of freedom to
explain the ambiguous nature of Kantian political reform. The foundation
of moral subjectivity discussed in chapter 1 is crucial to understanding the
purpose of justice. This is because the absolute autonomy of morals
demanded by Kantian subjectivity creates a necessary dualism in his
thought between morals and politics. The ontological alienation of the
latter from the requirements of the former ultimately causes injustice and
thus the requirement of political reform. Nonetheless, I have argued that
the two sides of freedom that Kant uses to articulate the principles of justice and the necessity of reform also contain ambiguity. Although external
freedom and therefore politics ostensibly receive their shape only from the
formal principles of internal freedom (that is, morals), it transpires that
Kant does not rigidly sustain this distinction. Thus, although Kantian justice would seem initially to suggest that the reform of politics requires
only a transcendence of the state of nature in order to secure equal

domains of external freedom, there are conflicting elements in his thought that suggest that justice requires the gradual but direct realization of a kingdom of ends in order to realize increased internal freedom or autonomy.

The one aspect of Kant's political theory that now requires elaboration is his doctrine of state sovereignty. For political reform depends upon the sovereign state; it is the mechanism that creates and implements the reality of external freedom. But the nature of Kant's commitment to the sovereign state is complicated by the bifurcation of freedom upon which his view of justice relies. Moreover, the context of international politics, in which there exists a plurality of sovereign agents, poses an additional and arguably unique challenge to Kantian justice that requires explanation.

CHAPTER 3

KANT, STATE SOVEREIGNTY, AND INTERNATIONAL REFORM

It is arguable that Kant accepts too much sovereignty for one who is arguing against Hobbes.

—Patrick Riley[1]

To Kant, the sovereignty of man is a political tragedy.

—Jens Bartelson[2]

For Kant, sovereignty is the key mechanism of political reform. It is the way in which politics can be domesticated to approximate the formal principles of morality. However, state sovereignty also presents Kant with a profound set of moral difficulties that ultimately threatens the realization of justice too. For, although sovereignty is a necessary cause of justice, it is also, paradoxically, a major cause of injustice both domestically and internationally. In this chapter I demonstrate that Kant's advocacy of international reform is consistent with, and a crucial part of, his general attempt to articulate the conditions of justice as a means by which individuals are empowered to eliminate if not reduce the large discrepancy between morality and politics.

The approach I adopt here is to reconstruct and categorize the many (often conflicting) statements that Kant makes on the concept of sovereignty, and—for the sake of convenience—call them his "doctrine" of sovereignty. I then interpret this paradoxical doctrine in light of the nature of Kantian justice discussed in the previous chapter. I argue that Kant's famous call for international reform is a product of the problematic role that sovereignty plays within realizing justice.

The first section is a detailed analysis of Kant's doctrine of sovereignty. Here I show that his view of sovereignty is often ambiguous because it rests on two distinct grounds: first, a "dogmatic" and *a priori* formal justification; and, second, a call to constantly reform the empirical existence of all sovereigns everywhere. The main finding of this analysis is that Kant's view of sovereignty is fundamentally dualistic because of the bifurcated structure upon which justice depends. The second section explains the genesis and nature of Kant's call for international reform found in "Perpetual Peace" through an examination of the justifications he employs, and mechanisms he proposes, to support such a project.

The justifications for international reform, especially those found in the "Doctrine of Right," are key because they point to a contradiction within sovereignty that potentially renders Kantian justice impossible, that is, sovereignty as a cause of both justice and injustice. In light of the findings of chapter 2, I then disentangle two distinct justifications of international reform that have, for the most part, been conflated by Kant scholars (an honest tendency given that Kant himself often does much the same thing). The first justification is entirely formal and is concerned only with injustice among sovereign states as agents; the second is concerned with removing the constraints imposed upon reform within states by the international context, and thus with the existence of injustice within states. In the former instance, reform of interstate relations is required for the exact same reasons that it was of individuals in the state of nature. Kant's argument here is entirely formal in that interstate reform is required by justice *qua* justice and its transcendental principles; thus sovereign states become the subjects of his theory of justice in a way that was only possible for individuals, that is, obligations are imposed upon them in order to balance and limit their freedom.

The second justification forwarded by Kant is not purely formal because it considers the negative consequences that international anarchy (and war) have upon the realization of justice within the state. Quite simply, he thinks that any freedom obtained by individuals within the sovereign state is liable to be insecure, incomplete, and incoherent as long as there is unmitigated anarchy among states. Within this justification, states are not the pure subjects of justice as much as they are tools that must be made adequate to the task of maximizing individual freedom; the purpose of international reform here is thus more clearly that of increasing justice for individuals rather than for states.

When considered together, these two justifications suggest something very important and arguably original for the time in which Kant lived: The conditions of justice at the international and domestic levels are, in fact, closely interrelated. I argue that because Kant's theory of justice gives priority to the formal principles over material ones, he is often led to suggest that states are analogous to individuals. However, it is the second, material, justification that serves as a more solid ground for political reform because true individual autonomy is more obviously served by its expression.

With respect to the question of how international reform is to occur according to Kant, I focus on two separate yet related mechanisms, both of which rely upon the existence of sovereign states. The difficulty with many accounts of Kant's position on international politics in "Perpetual Peace" is that they deal only with the mechanisms for reform without placing them in the context of Kantian justice. This can lead only to an incomplete or, worse, distorted account of the limits and possibilities of reform that Kant had in mind in 1795 and hence to anachronism on the part of modern interpreters. My argument in this section is that Kant's choice of mechanisms reflects the tensions between the differing justifications for reform. Although his purely formal justification of reform would seem to demand a global sovereign and the elimination of independent states, his material justification permits him to circumvent this necessity by pointing to the likely terrible consequences of such revolutionary transformation.

The mechanisms that Kant selects for reform suggest that, ultimately, his material principles of justice have a more prominent role in his international thought. This is because each of the two indicates that Kant is willing to tolerate the continued existence of the state of nature among states because they are likely to permit more individual freedom as imperfect tools of reform than would be in a world state. The agency of sovereign states is, as it is for domestic reform, the medium through which gradual changes to the phenomenal world of politics are to be best effected.

The first mechanism is the republican constitution, the only *form* of sovereignty that is, in Kant's view, capable of reconciling inner sovereignty with the state's exercise of external relations in a way that transcends the *effects* of anarchy. The second mechanism is Kant's concept of a teleological history. Although this process also relies upon the agency of sovereign states, it does so in spite of the particular aims and intentions of states. In the first mechanism, Kant implies that sovereign states are capable of self-reform. In the second, he concedes that such self-reform is unlikely given that it relies upon the discretion of sovereign states with little incentive or opportunity to reform under existing anarchic conditions. A teleological conception of history is thus crucial because it outlines a path by which sovereign states are pushed in the direction to which they are naturally averse: pacific relations in a federation of republican states that alleviates the insecurity and tyranny that Kant associates with anarchy. Although these two mechanisms suggest that Kant is willing to subordinate the formal requirement of a world state that his theory of justice ought to have rationally legislated, his materially inspired principles are arguably designed to have a formalizing effect on international relations. This is because the final aim of international reform is still only that of reconciling the freedom or external sovereignty of states, and not the imposition of ends upon each state.[3] This suggests that Kant himself does not take up the radical potential of his ethico-political philosophy in international politics.

KANT'S DOCTRINE OF STATE SOVEREIGNTY

In his study of sovereignty, F. H. Hinsley distinguishes its "internal" from its "external" dimensions. The former refers to the presence of an absolute authority within the state and consequent establishment of a domestic political order. The latter points to the absence of such an order among states and the subsequent anarchy that sovereignty thus creates. He claims that "[i]n theory this is not a paradoxical outcome but a logical consequence of the sovereignty concept."[4] By this reasoning, the internal and external sides of state sovereignty—and the juxtaposition of political society and interstate anarchy they create—are two sides of the same coin, a "logical" and necessary result of the concept.[5]

Kant recognizes, yet rejects as necessary, the "logical" results of sovereignty's division into internal and external. More specifically, although Kant recognizes that interstate anarchy is an inevitable result of state sovereignty, his commitment to justice leads him to suggest that there is a requirement—indeed, a moral duty—to attempt a reconciliation of internal and external sovereignty. In other words, on the basis of his understanding of justice, Kant claims there is a need to reform interstate relations just as there is a need to create civil society domestically.

Kant does not have a neatly articulated doctrine of state sovereignty in any single one of his texts. Thus any effort to contrive a coherent, systematic, and formally defended position on sovereignty risks reading into Kant a posture that he cannot have possibly agreed with or recognized.[6] In presenting a "doctrine" of sovereignty I intend merely to assemble the most salient attitudes that he expresses on this subject in order to clarify their place and meaning within his political philosophy. There are two very different types of statements on sovereignty in Kant's texts, each of which has different implications. One type posits an *a priori* necessity for an absolute sovereign agent that is beyond questioning; the other is a call to continuously reform all sovereign states everywhere in order to perfect their internal constitutions and, equally crucial, to transcend the effects of the anarchic condition among them. Both of these elements rely upon the demands of freedom and justice discussed in the previous chapters.

In the "Doctrine of Right," Kant posits the *a priori* necessity of an absolutist sovereign agent in the state.[7] This defense of sovereignty gives systematic definition to various statements in his other political writings to the effect that "man is *an animal who needs a master.*"[8] Now, this demand for sovereignty is made from pure practical reason, which means that sovereignty is demonstrated to be necessary from the *a priori* reasoning that transcends all possible experience.[9] "Man" needs a "master" because, in a world shared by individual agents, there can be no external freedom without an absolute will to ensure a legal-political framework for justice. For otherwise the individual "certainly abuses his freedom in relation to others of his own kind."[10] The inherent inclination of each individual to make an exception from universal principles of justice requires a sovereign enforcement agency. As Kant writes, a sovereign is needed "to break … [our] self-will and force [each] to obey a universally valid will under which everyone can be free."[11]

It is important to realize that Kant is not making an anthropological claim that individuals are empirically evil and thus need a Leviathan to produce order.[12] To the contrary, it is the transcendental argument that in a state of nature there can be no universally just condition. This is because, in the absence of a sovereign, "each has its own right to do *what seems right and good to it* and not to be dependent upon another's opinion on this."[13] Kant states that in such an anarchic condition freedom is impossible because of an absence of protection from the coercive imposition of one's will upon another. This situation is morally unacceptable because it negates our universal capacity to set and follow our own ends autonomously—the essence of our humanity.[14] Kant derives two unconditional duties from this realization: a duty of individuals to leave the state of nature and join civil society[15] and a duty to never resist the sovereign.[16] Both of these requirements involve the legitimate coercion of the individual to make his or her freedom compatible with the freedom of others.[17]

What is notable about Kant's *a priori* argument for sovereignty is its apparently dogmatic and absolutist character. He claims that the people must never question the historical origins or legislative legitimacy of the sovereign's will.[18] At one point he introduces the "principle that the presently existing legislative authority ought to be obeyed, whatever its origin."[19] Scholars have long wondered why, in addition to dogmatism, Kant relies on such an absolutist conception of sovereignty to underwrite his understanding of public legal justice.[20] Kant asserts that the sovereign is the supreme, *illimitable* power that is not subject to law or bound by legal duty.[21] It is famously known that—despite his admiration for the historical meaning of the French Revolution[22]—Kant refuses the right of rebellion to all peoples, no matter how grievously abusive and authoritarian the regime.[23]

Kant does not view his apology for an absolute and illimitable sovereign as "dogmatic" in a technical sense. Sovereignty is entirely consistent with the critical method of *a priori* reasoning and the morality of the categorical imperative.[24] There can be no coercion employed against the sovereign because it would negate entirely the transcendental system of justice. Opposing the sovereign would only destroy that which enables an escape from anarchy. As Nicholson states, for Kant, it would be contradictory and incoherent to think that it is "just to resist the source of justice."[25] Additionally, just as he opposes deceit and lies, Kant's objection to disobedience of the sovereign is rooted in a formal requirement of universalizability. Therefore, regardless of the consequences for which we might hope in opposing an unjust sovereign, resistance is forbidden because it makes the possibility of *any* civil constitution impossible when universalized. As he notes in "Perpetual Peace," "any *legal* constitution, even if it is only in small measure *lawful*, is better than none at all."[26] This suggests that all empirically existing states are compatible with freedom insofar as they are a bulwark against lawlessness.

There is however another side of Kant's doctrine of sovereignty. Alongside the statements noted above, there is an unmistakable and sustained call for the transformation and continual *reform* of sovereigns everywhere. The main reason for this seemingly contrary position is that—in spite of whatever *a priori* arguments exist in favor of sovereignty—the actual or phenomenal reality of sovereign power poses immense threats to human freedom. There is no shortage of evidence of this sentiment, but perhaps the most clear expression is this:

> In the face of the omnipotence of nature, or rather its supreme first cause which is inaccessible to us, the human being is, in his turn, but a trifle. But for the sovereigns of his own species to also consider him as such, whether by burdening him as an animal, regarding him as a mere tool of their designs, or exposing him in their conflicts with one another in order to have him massacred—this is no trifle, but a subversion of the purpose of creation itself.[27]

Here Kant acknowledges that it is not merely the lawlessness of the state of nature that is a threat to human freedom. The cure of sovereignty can be almost as bad as the disease called anarchy (though never, according to Kant, quite as bad).[28] For sovereigns are liable to treat their subjects as mere means rather than ends, thus negating the basis of humanity altogether. Moreover, the immoral situation of lawless anarchy is now reproduced *among* sovereign states, creating an endless incentive for war and the systematic negation of freedom that results from its outbreak. Thus, the enabling condition of justice inside of the state produces a situation of international injustice that demands reform.

Kant's doctrine of sovereignty becomes profoundly complicated by the question of political reform. The view that any empirically existing sovereign is a sufficient mechanism for freedom is now called into question. This is because he introduces an external *standard* for the reform of sovereignty—the "original contract"—that is a goal so lofty that no amount of political improvement could totally satisfy its requirements.[29] Similar to Rousseau's view of sovereignty, this Idea supports a legislator that wills *only* that which individuals would consent to, thus being entirely compatible with a society of autonomous or lawgiving members. According to Kant, no empirically existing sovereign is entirely adequate or compatible with freedom when judged against this standard. In the "Doctrine of Right" his absolutist statements on sovereign legitimacy are therefore closely followed by assertions on the necessity for reform toward the only constitution that can *approximate* the original contract, a republican constitution. As he writes:

> [T]he *spirit* of an original contract ... involves an obligation on the part of the constituting authority to make the *kind of government* suited to the system of an original contract. Accordingly, even if this cannot be done all at once, it is under obligation to change the kind of government gradually and continually so that it harmonizes *in its effect* with the only constitution that accords with right, that of a pure republic, in such a way that the old (empirical) statutory forms, which served merely to bring about the *submission* of the people, are replaced by the original (rational) form, the only form which makes *freedom* the principle and indeed the condition for any exercise of *coercion,* as is required by a rightful constitution of a state in the strict sense of the word.[30]

The constant reform of sovereignty required by the standard of an original contract is especially important for international politics because, as discussed below, once "domestic" anarchy is overcome by sovereignty, it is only the reform of sovereignty that can domesticate the international sphere.[31] A republican constitution ensures that the sovereign is made responsive to the ends of its citizens and is thus entirely cautious about its external conduct.

How can these two distinct types of statements that constitute Kant's doctrine of sovereignty be explained? A first step is to examine more closely those few occasions that he explicitly defines a "sovereign." Perhaps unsurprisingly, however, he uses two definitions. In the case of his dogmatic defense of sovereignty, Kant equates it merely with *any* existing legislative mechanism that transcends the state of nature.[32] There is no question of a constitutional division of powers within the state or of the requirement of consent by the people.[33] But the other definition of sovereignty in Kant's texts is predicated on the second, reformist element of the doctrine outlined above. Sovereignty is that which belongs "only to the united will of the people."[34] Under this definition the sovereign legislative agency is only one of three powers in a constitutionally divided state (the others being the executive and judiciary branches). Sovereignty is thus dependent here upon the restraints that Kant associates with the popular will.[35]

The differences between the two types of statements that constitute Kant's doctrine of sovereignty are paradoxical, but not necessarily contradictory. This is because of the dialectical, "top-down" nature of the reform process that he envisages. True to the logic of sovereignty, reform must be self-generated and entirely initiated by the sovereign itself: "A change in a (defective) constitution, which may certainly be necessary at times, can ... be carried out through *reform* by the sovereign itself, but not by the people ... ."[36] The "is" of the actually existing sovereign (found in the first definition above) must contain the seeds of the sovereign that "ought" to be (of the second definition). Kant's view is that once the sovereign creates a mere lawful "civil union" out of anarchy, it alone will have the force and legislative legitimacy to progressively re-create itself in history and to produce a "society" based increasingly on the just principles of the original contract.[37] The original contract is an Idea that we can only approximate in empirical reality. This means that the ideal of self-legislating citizens is approximated by the sovereign ruling *as if* the citizens were the ones who were truly sovereign. In other words, the discretion is with the sovereign to decide if the political community *could* rationally agree with its decision.[38] Kant's ever-changing empirical sovereign is, therefore, a surrogate for the aspiration of an authentically "popular" sovereign. As Pogge notes, under Kant's principle of Right, "[i]t is juridically permissible to maintain an inferior instantiation [of the constitution], and juridically impermissible for citizens to obstruct the sovereign's efforts to do so."[39]

Until now I have described only the main elements of Kant's dualistic doctrine of sovereignty and suggested how they are related to one another. In the main, I have abstracted Kant's attitude toward sovereignty from his theory of justice in order to highlight its essential dualism. However, in order to explain this dualism, sovereignty must be placed within his ethico-political thought. Most generally, Kant's position on state sovereignty is shaped by his vision of subordinating politics—to the greatest extent possible—to an autonomous morality. However, the chasm between morals and politics in Kant's political thought that I have explored in the previous chapters complicates his view of sovereignty: His doctrine of sovereignty is dualistic and ambiguous because it is justified by his bifurcated concept of freedom and the tensions produced by its formal and material requirements.

The justification of Kant's absolutist and dogmatic statements on sovereignty is rather straightforward. As anarchy is always the antithesis of freedom, the sovereign state is necessitated by the requirements of external freedom. All lawless forms of coercion must be supplanted with a mechanism of lawful and legitimate coercion of a single agent. This agent, the sovereign, creates and enforces the necessary conditions of consistent domains of external freedom only. Because of this, sovereignty is directly justified only by a *formal* cause, as opposed to any possible *material* consequences. This consideration is extremely important because it means that state sovereignty is necessary *in spite of its consequences*. This stance is consistent with Kant's deontological ethics. However, as we shall see, Kant realizes perfectly that there are problematic consequences posed by the empirical existence of sovereign states. These negative results, however, are superseded in importance by the formal or transcendental framework that justifies freedom.

The second, reformist element of Kant's doctrine of sovereignty has a more complicated justification. It is necessary to recall Kant's distinction between internal and external individual freedom in addition to the formal and material demands upon which they are based. Kant immediately realizes the tragic (material) consequences of any commitment to state sovereignty. The state's internal sovereignty is compatible with the (formal) requirements of external freedom, but these requirements are immediately threatened by the production of international anarchy. The immoral condition of anarchy that necessitated the (formal) justification of the sovereign state is (materially) *re-created* among sovereign states with no global authority to arbitrate differences. In other words, the (formal) requirement of individual external freedom creates internal sovereignty; but the (material) result of interstate anarchy is something (formally) forbidden by Kant's political theory. Anarchy should be no less a moral problem among states for Kant than it is among individuals, and hence he realizes that there is a conflict between the (formal) requirements of external liberty inside the state and the (formal) requirements of just international politics. Thus, Kant realizes perfectly the "paradox" of sovereignty to which Hinsley alludes, between its internal and external dimensions. However, he rejects the necessity of this paradox because it would place the (formal) requirements of external freedom in contradiction. The political solution to this problem, as we shall see, is the reform of the empirically existing sovereign state into the only type that Kant thinks can reconcile its internal and external sovereignty to transcend the effects of anarchy, that is, a republican constitution.

What is frequently overlooked or minimized by interpretively conservative scholars of Kant's political and international theory are the important material incentives for reform.[40] As I claimed in the previous chapter, although material incentives related to internal freedom and enlightenment are of secondary importance when compared to the formal realm of external freedom, they are still profound. Sovereignty is clearly in need of reform for Kant because its empirical existence is potentially a constant threat to the inner autonomy of individuals and their progress as rational, self-actualized beings. The wars that emanate from the clash of sovereigns in anarchy require states to commit what morality forbids—the strategic use of its citizens as mere instruments for the state's survival. Indeed, the immoral consequences of war is a theme that is most striking in many of Kant's writings.[41]

The requirements and restrictions engendered by Kant's division between the internal and the external sides of individual freedom thus justify both the sovereign state *and* its necessary reform. Reform of the existing sovereign state is justified not only by the formal requirements of individual freedom, but also by its material requirements. Nonetheless, this reform project is not limited to the domestic sphere, but is necessarily international in scope.

KANT'S INTERNATIONAL REFORM PROJECT AND JUSTICE

Kant proposes an international reform project. Although this project is essential to the realization of justice, its particular nature is also a consequence of his problematic and dualistic doctrine of state sovereignty. In this section I explain Kant's aspirations for international reform by reconstructing his arguments that justify its necessity, and, subsequently, by interpreting the mechanisms of reform contained in "Perpetual Peace."

Kant's vision of reforming politics to approximate the formal principles of morality cannot arbitrarily end at the boundaries of the sovereign state—it necessarily applies to all politics. Nevertheless, the fundamental dualism animating Kantian justice affects the extent to which the international sphere is brought under the sovereign control of an autonomous morality. The ensuing analysis places two justifications and two mechanisms for international reform within the conceptual framework of the previous chapter and the conflicting demands that Kant makes of sovereignty analyzed directly above. It transpires that there is ambiguity about the essential purpose of international reform: Although there are suggestions that such reform is about the *domestication* of sovereign states (in the way that individuals were brought under control within the state), Kant ends up advocating merely a *reconciliation* of sovereign states. This is a consequence not only of the separate justifications he makes for reform, but of the two distinct mechanisms that he advocates for its accomplishment.

The Justification of Reform

In his provocative essay "Why Is There No International Theory?" Martin Wight argues that there is a lack of serious theoretical reflection on interstate relations in the history of Western thought. He suggests that a true *theory* of politics may be possible only when there is a perceived chance of realizing some Good, or of at least achieving some progress in its direction.[42] Because the anarchy created by the independence of states prevents the achievement of such things in any meaningful sense internationally, the limits of reformative measures coincide with the boundaries among states. Accordingly, claims Wight, international *theory* is merely a weak and diffuse set of insights, unable to constitute a reality in which interstate *practice* is made compatible with any conception of the Good.[43] Wight's statements affirm an ontological difference between domestic and international spheres, the latter being extremely recalcitrant to progressive transformation.

Like Wight, Kant assumes that international politics is different from domestic politics in that its reform is far more difficult to achieve with the absence of an overarching global sovereign. Also like Wight, Kant is skeptical about—if not outright opposed to—the imposition of any conception of a universal Good onto a pluralistic interstate order.[44] Nonetheless, Kant could not disagree more with a thinker such as Wight about the relationship between international theory and practice—especially when it comes to achieving a condition of interstate justice or Right—something that is entirely distinct from the Good. Quite simply, Wight assumes the same thing that Kant thinks is all too common among students of international politics—men such as Grotius, Pufendorf and Vattel. Wight and these earlier philosophers assume that theory on the relations among states (or any politics for that matter) must conform with practice. It is this point, no doubt, that Kant had in mind when he criticized the three prior to his time as "sorry comforters."[45] In light of the autonomy-of-morals foundation, however, Kant holds that theory must legislate the conditions of political practice if it is to be coherent and supportive of justice.

As argued above, Kant holds that political practice must be subordinated as much as possible to formal principles that are derived from
reason rather than from experience. When one looks merely at interstate
practice to guide *theoretical* principles of how states ought to act, it is no
small wonder that international theory would appear rather primitive if
compared with politics within the state. This is because, principally,
the absence of a global sovereign invariably renders political dynamics
empirically different than external relations among individuals in states.
However, Kant does not think that this material reality indicates any inherent and necessary ontological difference between domestic and international politics. On the contrary, he argues that all relationships between
autonomous agents must be considered from the standpoint of universal
principles of Right: There is thus "an absolute and primary duty in all
external relationships whatsoever among human beings who cannot avoid
mutually influencing each other" to submit to principles of justice.[46] By
referring to "all" external relationships here he includes those of sovereign
states. Thus, the mere fact of difference between international and domestic realms, caused by state sovereignty, is, from the standpoint of Kantian
justice, largely irrelevant. We cannot be satisfied to merely domesticate and
reform politics within the state and permit anarchy to reign outside of its
boundaries.

Kantian international reform is justified in the first instance by a simple application of the purely *formal* principles of his theory of justice from
individuals in the state of nature to sovereign states in global anarchy.
Paradoxically, of course, the very requirement of justice among states is a
product of the existence of those sovereign agents that Kant claims are
absolutely necessary for justice among individuals. Under this justification, it is states—and not individual beings—that are the proper and
relevant subjects of international justice. Kant relies here on a "domestic
analogy" because the experience of reform within the state is logically
applied to the international level simply because of an assumption that all
political relations must be domesticated by the same logic of universal,
constitutional relations found within the ideal of an original contact.[47]

Laberge argues that, on the basis of Kantian justice, Kant's "ideal
theory" of international relations would unquestionably demand a global
sovereign to act as a mechanism of justice.[48] Pogge, too, claims that from
the purely formal dimensions of justice, Kant could point only in such
a direction.[49] Both note, however, that Kant explicitly rejects this avenue
of reform because he views it as tantamount to a "soulless despotism."
Thus, Kant himself imposes crucial limits on the entirely formal demands
of his theory of justice in international politics; and, as a result, his use

of the "domestic analogy" breaks down. Given Kant's doctrine of sovereignty explained above, the global sovereign rationally prescribed by international justice would need to be an absolute and illimitable agent. Such an agent could exist only if the sovereignty of existing states were eliminated. Thus, given the dogmatism of Kant's view of sovereignty, international justice based on a purely formal justification would require a revolutionary alteration to the status quo—it would require that existing relationships between citizens and sovereigns in all particular states be terminated, and that all rightful external relationships among individuals be enforced by the global sovereign. Kant rejects this eventuality by supplementing his view of international reform with a much more subtle justification.

In my view, Kant's second justification is arguably conditioned by the latent *material* elements of his theory of justice. This justification is different from the first because, rather than being concerned with the mere existence of anarchy, it is instead concerned with the *consequences* of anarchy—especially for the realization of justice for actual individuals within existing sovereign states. Anarchy among states needs to be reformed because it is a detriment to the realization of reform within states; Kant thinks that any freedom obtained by individuals within the sovereign state is rendered incoherent and insecure as long as war is possible among states. Thus the domestic and international realms are logically linked: "The problem of establishing a perfect civil constitution is subordinate to the problem of a law-governed external relationship with other states, and cannot be solved unless the latter is also solved."[50] This suggests that the strategic pressures caused by anarchy create a nearly irresistible incentive to delay and stifle any reform of sovereigns within states. The formal conditions of justice, viz., the realization of external liberty among individuals, is thus always contingent upon international politics.

Kant thus goes beyond a merely formal justification for international reform because a far more crucial and pressing incentive is the citizen's liberty. Unlike the first justification, states are not the only relevant subjects of international justice because the ultimate purpose of political reform is individual freedom. As he claims, "[T]he hiring of men to kill or be killed seems to mean using them as mere machines and instruments in the hands of someone else (the state), which cannot be easily reconciled with the rights of man in one's own person."[51] This concern is articulated somewhat differently in the "Doctrine of Right," where he notes:

> For they [i.e., individuals] must always be regarded as co-legislating members of a state (not merely as means but also as ends in themselves), and must therefore give their free assent, through their representatives, not only

to waging war in general but also to each particular declaration of war. Only under this limiting condition can a state direct them to serve in a way full of danger to them.[52]

He also writes that within the context of international anarchy, sovereigns feel justified in wasting material resources on war preparations that might otherwise be used to improve the cultural conditions and well-being of peoples.[53] Kant intimates that the moral realization of autonomous individuals is negatively affected by the wasted material resources spent on wars, and thus his often expressed view that internal freedom is not connected to the phenomenal world of politics is transcended. States are unable to perfect their formal constitutions in a state of war, and, moreover, they must use their citizens as fodder. Thus, if states are the principal subjects of international justice, it is simply because they are (problematic) tools or mechanisms in the service of individual freedom. Kant is here implicitly rejecting a simplistic and overly formal domestic analogy that his first justification would have required on its own.

A crucial effect of this second, material justification of international reform is that within his posited interrelation of domestic and international justice, the closest and most pragmatic fit between the individual's freedom and sovereignty is at the state level. His rejection of a suprastate and global sovereign takes this material cause as a point of departure. States are certainly imperfect tools of justice in need of reform, but this reform should be allowed to proceed as much as possible in the context of an international anarchy that is progressively civilized by a pragmatic alternative to world government. As we shall see, this mechanism is a federation of republican states.

If the reformist element of Kant's doctrine of sovereignty discussed above is contingent upon the production of freedom, international reform is rooted within the same set of moral concerns. Kant advocates international reform in order to reconcile the internal and the external sides of sovereignty. This reconciliation aims primarily to overcome the contradiction between the realization of the formal principles of justice within the state and the lack of the same among states. Thus there is a combination of formal and material causes rooted in the transcendental goal of freedom that justifies international reform. The justification of international reform in Kant's thinking is complex. On the one hand, international reform is a necessity simply because of injustice, that is, sovereign states in a state of nature. This justification would be entirely formal and based on a strict domestic analogy in which states are imbued with the same characteristics as individuals and require a global sovereign. Ultimately, however, his use of such an analogy is weakened because of the fear of a world government. Rather than eliminating independent states, international reform becomes depicted as a matter of reconciling internal and external sovereignty.

The strict use of a domestic analogy breaks down in Kant's thought for two key reasons. First, the internal freedom of individuals is fundamentally unlike the internal sovereignty of states—it is a purely moral or noumenal realm that is unaffected by politics. Second, the balancing of the external freedom of individuals within the state requires a sovereign agent, one that is unavailable and undesirable among states. Nonetheless, I think international reform is also justified by Kant in order to alleviate certain material, phenomenal conditions that would render the realization of justice within the state impossible. Here states are not so much akin to individuals in the state of nature so much as they are the problematic tools of reform that need to be tamed and transformed in the name of realizing individual freedom. Thus Kant slips back and forth between two justifications: one that appeals to justice *qua* justice as the ultimate ground for change in the way that states interact as legal persons and another that views states less as subjects of international justice than the *cause* of injustice domestically when wars are imposed upon individuals.

The genesis and justification of Kant's international reform project have been located in the problematic terms of his own doctrine of sovereignty. The goal is to reconcile the internal and external sides of sovereignty—but this project is merely a part of Kant's overall desire to articulate the conditions under which politics may be made compatible with morality. Nonetheless, international reform is distinct from intrastate reform only because, although the agency of the state is still central, the domestication of anarchy does not involve a global sovereign. Instead, Kant forwards two related yet distinct mechanisms for international reform that serve as a substitute for one.

The Mechanisms of Reform

"Perpetual Peace" is Kant's programmatic statement on international reform. Although it contains many indications of the ethico-political justifications for such reform, the main contribution of this essay is the elaboration of mechanisms by which international change is to occur. These mechanisms are misunderstood if they are interpreted out of context—more specifically, the Kantian position on international politics cannot be properly explained only through this essay because the essay lacks a systematic account of his view of justice. Accordingly, I shall subordinate the mechanisms found in "Perpetual Peace" to the above interpretation of Kantian justice as it is presented in the *Metaphysics of Morals*.

Kant divides the essay into six preliminary articles, three definitive articles, two supplements, and a two-part appendix. If "Perpetual Peace" is designed to be a hypothetical peace treaty among states, it is scarcely a conventional example of the type of document that the governments and diplomats of real states might themselves construct. As many modern commentators note, the prescriptions Kant made in 1795 are remarkably prescient in that they anticipate the efforts of international organization in our time.[54] However, there has also been plenty of anachronism and distortion, too, among modern commentators that read into Kant certain tendencies that clearly exceed his intentions and the limitations he imposed upon the nature of international reform. This matter will receive sustained attention in subsequent chapters.

In this section I explain the two principal mechanisms of reform advocated in "Perpetual Peace" by situating them within two types of justifications analyzed above. The mechanisms Kant articulates are a consequence of his realization that his "ideal theory" of international politics, to use Laberge's term, is a nonstarter. A purely formal theory of international justice would require a global sovereign as the *only* mechanism adequate to the task of domesticating the state of nature among states. Kant thus relaxes the formal demands of international justice by nominating states as useful tools that have, he claims, achieved *some* degree of justice within them and thus merit the opportunity to further their trajectories toward internal perfection. Thus a material justification for reform ultimately supersedes his purely formal one. As a consequence, the two most salient mechanisms that he actually advocates reflect the special agency he ascribes to sovereign states in order to accomplish a minimal agenda. This agenda is not to completely domesticate anarchy—but only to reduce its problematic *effects*. Rather than abolishing anarchy, the aim of international reform is limited to that of reconciling the sovereignty of states such that their free choices do not result in the outbreak of wars that would violate the humanity of their citizens. As Laberge suggests, the mechanisms that Kant explicitly endorses thus constitute a "nonideal" theory of international relations.[55]

What is key in the mechanisms discussed below is that, like reform within domestic society, nearly all progressive change is channeled through the agency of the sovereign (or in this case, the plurality of sovereigns). The nonideal theory thus enshrines the sovereignty of states as a given foundation of international order, a commitment expressed clearly in "Perpetual Peace"'s preliminary articles.[56] It is a nonideal theory because, when reform rests upon the discretion of states, the process becomes dependent upon a highly contingent and difficult set of conditions that cannot be achieved without painful episodes of war. Nevertheless, Kant hopes that the progress of reforms toward justice within certain states will provide the impetus of realizing the limited form of international justice he ultimately advocates. If the two mechanisms discussed below thus rely upon the agency of sovereigns, the crucial difference between them pertains to the question of whether states intentionally *will* the reform of their interrelations or whether they are pushed into it by history *qua* nature.

Mechanism One: Republics Inside/Confederalism Outside   As Nicholas Greenwood Onuf has written, the republican legacy is a complex part of Western political and international theory.[57] For the ancients, a republic was the shared experience of any political association. The interplay of natural and conventional conditions that made this experience "good" was its "constitution." Onuf suggests that the republican tradition holds that common ends and purposes take precedence over individual autonomy and agency. However, this changes in modernity with the rise of individual subjectivity. Republicanism is no longer viewed as an intrinsic characteristic of the entire political community, but only as a form of government in the sovereign state that is clearly set apart from civil society. When Kant speaks of a republic, he is using this modern sense, even though he hopes this form of government will serve the "general will" (a term he uses to refer to the common good—something to which all independent citizens could conceivably consent).

The first mechanism that Kant advocates for international reform is the republican constitution. This corresponds logically to his view that the cause of war is the improper location of sovereignty in the state. As will be explored in subsequent chapters, Kant anticipates a long line of liberals by claiming that the "location" of sovereignty within the state has a decisive effect on war.[58] That is, conflict arises from some "flaws" in the organization of domestic society and the particular state. Just as he contests the location of the true grounds of human agency in the amoral or material causes of subjectivity, Kant has very specific views on where the internal sovereignty of states ought to be placed.

The first two definitive articles of "Perpetual Peace" rely on the mechanism of the republican sovereign state as the agent of reform. We learned above that only a state that is reforming itself toward republican principles can reconcile the freedom of its citizens with the coercion required to produce a lawful society. Kant *internalizes* the freedom-promoting effects of republican regimes because he claims they are the only ones capable of pacifying international politics. In the first definitive article, he claims that when states are constitutionally divided between the executive and legislative branches of government, they are republican.[59] It does not matter if a state is formally ruled by a monarch or an elected ruler—as long as it is the citizens who legislate foreign policy decisions through their representatives, the state is actually republican. It is one of his more well known claims that "[i]f, as is inevitably the case under this constitution, the consent of the citizens is required to decide whether or not war is to be declared, it is very natural that they will have great hesitation in embarking on so dangerous an enterprise."[60]

Although it is the citizens who decide whether to go to war in a republican constitution, this reform of international anarchy that Kant has in mind is still a "top-down" mechanism. The first definitive article records his rejection of (direct) democracy as "necessarily a *despotism*"[61] because it collapses the distinction between legislative and executive branches of government and, moreover, negates the free choice of individuals by giving untempered power to an absolute majority.[62] Far more importantly, as we know from above, Kant's sovereign is ultimately indivisible and illimitable—it is not necessarily bound or (by his own vision of justice) required to act on the will of the people, only *as if* the people could consent to its decision.[63] The "original contract" that republican constitutions approximate is, after all, merely an Idea of reason.[64]

The second definitive article advocates the creation of a *confederation* of republican states. Kant initially uses an analogy of domestic politics to describe its intent: "Peoples who have grouped themselves into nation states may be judged in the same way as individual men living in the state of nature, independent of external laws; for they are a standing offence to one another by the very fact that they are neighbours."[65] This statement is occasionally taken with similar ones to imply that Kant advocates a League of Nations that has some kind of status, majesty, or power independent of the sovereign states that might be members. That is, just as Kant's doctrine of *internal* state sovereignty requires the presence of a legislative will over and above the wills of individuals, we would expect that he also supports a similar agent to perform much the same function among states. As Hinsley notes, however, Kant's view of federalism in the second definitive article is not akin to the domestic experience.[66] Kant's federalism is actually determined by the particular justifications he employs for international reform. Because he ultimately rejects a purely formal, ideal theory of international justice, his federalism is a surrogate for world government. It is a second-best mechanism because justice among states must in the end be subordinate to justice among individuals; for states are only the rational tools that we have created to enable and then maximize our external freedom.

Kant describes the development and form of his peace federation in a way that actually reaffirms the centrality of the (republican) sovereign state as the primary instrument of international reform. In a condition of anarchy, there is ultimately little opportunity or incentive for states to concede or limit their sovereign powers to defend themselves. As a result, a state *qua* state is unlikely to enter into anything more than an extraordinarily loose league: "[A] state which is self-governing and free from all external laws will not let itself become dependent upon the judgment of other states in seeking to uphold its rights against them."[67] This is comparable to Kant's statements that, in the state of nature among individuals, each is within his own right to rely on his own opinion of what is just and to further coerce the other to respect this power.[68] What this again suggests is that Kant is far more willing to tolerate anarchy among states than among individuals, in spite of his formal understanding of justice.

After many wars and failed attempts to secure peace, it will require the efforts of "one enlightened and powerful republic"[69] to establish pacific relations with its like-minded neighbors to create conditions favorable to a peaceful confederation. The confederation is ultimately limited, however, by the discrete inclinations and free choices of the sovereigns who have joined. Each member state may finally decide to exempt itself from the whole and, moreover, choose to dissolve the association at any time. If they are true republics, however—and this is obviously a big and important "if"—this voluntary nature of association is not a problem: States will be responsive to the pacific ends of citizens. Kant is very clear that sovereign states, as *representatives* (and mere tools) of their citizens, cannot be transferred to a transcendent suprastate. The confederation he proposes aims only for peaceful relations, not the construction of an "international state":[70] "A League of Nations in accordance with the idea of an original social contract is necessary, not in order to meddle in one another's internal dissensions but to protect attacks from without."[71]

Kant's reference to the original contract here is interesting because it again seems to render the relations among states as analogous to justice among individuals. Nevertheless, an interstate federalism is deemed essentially unlike the realization of the contract within the state because states "have already a lawful internal constitution ... [and they have] outgrown the coercive right of others to subject them to a wider legal constitution in accordance with their conception of right."[72] The existence of a suprastate would thus destroy the grounds of individual freedom because it would sever the assumed representative relationship between citizens and the sovereign.[73] This is additional evidence that the second, material justification trumps the initially pure formalism of Kant's first justification of international reform.

A significant implication of Kant's mechanism of the republican constitution is that, by itself, it suggests that individual external freedom is compatible with state sovereignty (even with the "international problem," i.e., anarchy). This is because the state with a republican constitution is viewed as essentially capable of willing self-reform in conjunction with other republics. The location of sovereignty in the united will of a people in each state reconciles the contradiction between their internal and external sovereignty. It is crucial to underscore that, in this mechanism, all reform—and by the same token its absence—is at the discretion of the sovereigns. Moreover, it is *intentional*. The particular and individual sovereign must eventually recognize the long-term rationality of reform. On this point Kant writes that "above all else a good will prepared to accept the findings of this experience" is needed.[74]

Even Kant's international confederation is entirely dependent upon the deliberate will of sovereign states. Just as the sovereign rules domestically *as if* the citizens could consent to the legislation of any particular policy,[75] the confederation envisaged here is merely a surrogate or "substitute" for a real global sovereign (that would be demanded by Kant's theory of justice if states were formally conceived as individuals).[76] Kant's criticism of Grotius, Pufendorf, and Vattel now seems overly harsh because he has left a remarkably wide latitude for states to define by themselves the practical terms of international reform. He appears to be a "sorry comforter" rather than the revolutionary cosmopolitan that his purely formal justification for international reform would require. It is quite possible that by leaving international reform to the discretion of sovereigns, Kant ends up with a kind of autonomy of politics by default.

Mechanism Two: The Idea of a Universal History   There are crucial limits to Kant's conviction regarding the capacities of sovereign states, even republican ones, to reform themselves. In the *Metaphysics of Morals* and scattered in his essays there are indications that he realized that the mislocation of sovereignty within the state is not the only, or even most important, cause of war and international injustice. To some extent, the reasons for this are similar to his position on individual subjectivity noted in chapter 1. Even if we relocate the ultimate ground of subjectivity in our rational moral capacities, individuals still exist in the empirical or phenomenal world. We are therefore inescapably conditioned by a worldly context and are thus subject to inclinations and self-interested calculations. Equally, even if we locate the sovereignty of the state in the citizens, republican states are in a phenomenal context, namely anarchy, that renders self-reform a tremendously difficult (yet entirely necessary) struggle. But here is where the similarity ends. Whereas individuals have a sovereign state to prevent them from acting consistently on their natural inclinations to the detriment of others, states have no such authority above them. Because states are free to judge their own disputes with one another, that is, because there is no *enforced* legal restrictions on their action, international politics remain an anarchic "state of war."[77]

Although Kant apparently criticizes any acceptance of the status quo of interstate anarchy (again, as "sorry comfort"), he actually condones as unavoidable the strategic reactions of states within this context: "[U]nless one neighbor gives a *guarantee* to the other at his request [to refrain from aggression] (which can only happen in a *lawful* state), the latter may treat him as an enemy."[78] Indeed, because Kant claims that no state is obliged to be a self-negating pacifist,[79] he as a philosopher must supply another "guarantee" for peace where states are unwilling or unable to do so themselves. This guarantee is the mechanism of nature *qua* history.

As Hannah Arendt notes, Kant has two distinct understandings of nature.[80] In one sense, the one assumed in chapter 1 above, nature is merely the opposite of moral or rational causality. Here nature is a system of prior causes that shapes and determines all phenomenal beings. Moreover, this system is entirely indifferent, if not hostile, to human purposes and the species' moral development. By contrast, Kant's second conception of nature is markedly different and coterminous with human history. Here nature is a teleological system of purposes that uses the phenomenal realm to realize the progress of the noumenal world in time. Kant's second understanding of nature is thus a quasi-phenomenology of human evolution. This is because, contrary to his purely formal moral-political framework, the material principles and natural inclinations that we know all too well from concrete experience now have an important and progressive role. Thus, even though Kant always insists that the ultimate grounds of human agency remain concealed and spontaneous because they lie within the realm of noumena, he also claims it is possible to determine the causes of behavior on a species-wide level from the standpoint of phenomena. The stimuli of human action from such a phenomenal point of view do not overstep the bounds of experience, "no matter how deeply concealed their [noumenal] causes may be."[81] Given Kant's critical epistemology, he does not think that history as mere events caused by human behavior is inherently progressive. "Yet," he claims, "if it may be *assumed* that nature does not work without a plan and purposeful end, even amidst the arbitrary play of human freedom, this idea may nevertheless prove useful."[82] Thus the mechanism of nature is progressive because it is a *regulative* Idea that can be used to judge or mediate the meaning of such events in light of the moral goals that we are unconditionally required to pursue. The philosopher needs to "discover a *purpose in nature* behind the senseless course of human events and decide whether it is possible after all to formulate in terms of a definite plan of nature a history of creatures who act without a plan of their own."[83] Even though nature is not truly a providential artist with the inherent goal of perfecting the human species, "we can and must *supply it mentally*" with such an aim.[84]

The fourth proposition of Kant's "The Idea for a Universal History with a Cosmopolitan Purpose" suggests how the mechanism of history operates: "The means which nature employs to bring about the development of the innate capacities [of the species] is that of antagonism within society, in so far as this antagonism becomes the long run cause of a law governed social order."[85] Kant also refers to this means as the dialectic of "unsocial sociability." The gulf between phenomenal human nature ("warped wood"[86]) and moral rationality that exists within each of us serves to transform the external relationships among us. If nature (in the first sense) directs us to serve our inclinations and act on material causes, then reason is our innate capacity (given to us by nature in the second sense) to transcend human nature and obey formal causes and universal laws. By nature (as mechanism), individuals are likely to act only on material principles of self-interest until reason legislates they act on formal principles of obligation. What history does, however, is allow our flaws to contribute to our perfection:

> And as far as reason is concerned, the result is the same as if man's selfish tendencies were non-existent, so that man, even if he is not morally good in himself, is nevertheless compelled to be a good citizen. As hard as it may sound, the problem of setting up a state can be solved even by a nation of devils (so long as they possess understanding) ... the mechanism of nature can be applied to all men in such a manner that the antagonism of their hostile attitudes will make them compel one another to submit to coercive laws, thereby producing a condition of peace within which the laws can be enforced.[87]

In "Perpetual Peace" Kant extends the influence of this mechanism from the realm of domestic society to relations among states. As Laberge writes, given the constraints of anarchy that Kant largely accepts, "[O]ne understands why, so as not to despair, Kant needed a philosophy of history according to which nature brings nations where they do not want to go."[88] The same dialectic of unsocial sociability among individuals can be viewed among states, and not merely by analogy. The "guarantee" of perpetual peace *is* history because states under conditions of anarchy will certainly seek to exempt themselves from obligations to other states merely by asserting their sovereignty. This mere assertion of absolute negative freedom will cause disagreement and violent conflict. The results of such natural expressions of self-interest eventually engender rational commitment to pursue formal obligations to other states. States are slowly led by the folly of their own short-term inclinations into the international confederation.

What is the relationship among republicanism, federalism, and a progressive history? Clearly the sovereign state is the agent of reform in both mechanisms. What sets apart the second, historical mechanism is that states reform in spite of their intentions and desires, just as rational individual devils within the state are able to transform their external conduct. Kant thus demonstrates a large degree of distrust and skepticism that states are capable of self-reform for international justice and individual freedom. This stance clearly contradicts the implicit optimism in the state that animates his first mechanism. The regulative Idea of a progressive history obviates the need for Kant to worry about the lack of faith he ultimately has in sovereigns to perceive their rational obligations.

Thus, the interconnection of the two mechanisms flows from the agency Kant ascribes to sovereigns in achieving international reform. They are the subjects of the moral learning immanent in the dialectic of history. It is only when they have experienced traumatic wars and reach complete "inner" exhaustion that particular sovereigns will finally "take the step which reason could have suggested to them even without so many sad experiences."[89] Kant even goes so far as to say that states are thus led, "even against their will, to enter into a cosmopolitan *constitution*."[90] What this suggests is that in spite of the essentially statist framework for change dictated by the terms of his understanding of justice, Kant views international reform as part and parcel of his general plan of reforming politics for the sake of morals. Because, as we know, justice is not limited to purely formal principles, he suggests several times that the end goal of international reform is to create as best approximation as is possible for the kingdom of ends prescribed by morality. In this approximation, "[t]he peoples of the earth have thus entered into varying degrees into a universal community, and it has developed to the point where a violation of rights in *one* part of the world is felt *everywhere*."[91] By reconciling the contradiction between internal and external state sovereignty, Kant envisages a political way to realize moral goals, all without—he hopes—sacrificing the essential autonomy of morals.

CONCLUSION

State sovereignty is arguably the key instrument for realizing Kantian justice. But the ambiguous nature of this justice renders his doctrine of sovereignty dualistic. The dualism of sovereignty is also evident in Kant's international reform project—a project required by the threat to justice *qua* justice by the mere existence of sovereign states. The formal elements of Kantian justice contribute to a "dogmatic" conception of an illimitable and absolute sovereign within the state and, ironically, to the necessity of a global sovereign that would domesticate and quash the independence of particular states. The material elements of justice, however, contribute to his "reformist" conception of a republican state that is open to the demands and claims of citizens and, internationally, to the reconciliation of external sovereignty via a universalization of republicanism and the development of a confederation of such states. Moreover, in both spheres, the international and the domestic, Kant hopes that the formal and material principle of justice will be realized in a progressive history.

In the main, Kant's doctrine of state sovereignty ought to strike the contemporary ear as antiquated, authoritarian, and profoundly illiberal. But its reformist elements, including that of international reform, have proved to be rather popular among advocates of a particular modern ideology—liberal internationalism. However, the foundations of Kant's political thought, especially his visions of subjectivity and justice, have not been adequately understood or criticized sufficiently by present-day exponents of Kantian peace plans. The extent to which all of these problematic foundations have been (uncritically) absorbed and reproduced in the liberal tradition is the subject of the ensuing chapters.

CHAPTER 4

LIBERAL INTERNATIONALISM AND THE KANTIAN "LEGACY"

The international arena has been the laboratory for testing liberal
political ideas since their invention, and what happens in it seems to
be that the government of real political entities is incompatible with
a clear notion of human autonomy ...

—Richard Tuck[1]

Since the end of the Cold War there has been a reascendancy of liberal
ideology and of liberal internationalist conceptions of politics.[2] The
apparent renewal in the 1990s of international organizations, international law, democracy, and free-market principles around the world has
put *realpolitik* on the defensive.[3] But liberal internationalism's revival is
not a monolithic or unchallenged phenomenon. Indeed, there are signs of
division among liberals too over the means and ends of international
peace, justice, and most fundamentally, individual freedom.

In this chapter I argue that the deepest division within liberal internationalism concerns the sovereign state and its ethical capacities. On the
one hand, a dominant sentiment in the tradition is that sovereign states
are the essential guarantors of liberty and can be reformed successfully to
promote universal liberal goals. On the other, there is an equally important (but less influential) countervailing skepticism within liberalism
broadly conceived. Quite simply, states have proved unable to promote
and protect freedom precisely because they have jealously retained their
sovereignty and have used it against universal interests. The decisive point
of contention is, therefore, whether sovereign states can be trusted with

our liberty and autonomy given the international problems of anarchy, war, and violence. As I show, the different liberal answers to this question directly inform alternative conceptions of international justice: that is, whether such justice consists primarily of reconciling the external sovereignty of states or, more ambitiously, requires the direct promotion of individual autonomy globally.

Interestingly, a nearly unanimous item of agreement is that Kant is a foundational source of the liberal internationalist tradition and can be invoked to support present-day liberal efforts to explain and to justify international and global reform. But Kant's actual texts do not provide as clear and uncontroversial a foundation as many would like; indeed, the already ambiguous statements he makes about sovereignty, justice, and international politics can be absorbed selectively to support rival liberalisms. Thus it is no small wonder that Kant's *legacy* has become a matter of competing Kantian *legacies*.

This chapter first explains the nature of liberal internationalism in relation to the dilemma of realizing individual freedom through sovereign states ostensibly located in anarchy. Here I explain the divisions within this tradition by referring to the different strategies that have been prescribed by liberals to promote its universalistic goals across interstate boundaries. For the most part, statist solutions dominate the tradition with only the occasional political crisis giving rise to nonstatist sentiments. The second and third sections explain the ethico-political and ideological reasons for Kant's inclusion within the liberal internationalist tradition, by both statist and nonstatist liberals. There are two reasons for Kant's ultimately contentious depiction as a founding father. First, his international reform project lends itself naturally to conflicting interpretations. Kant's bifurcated stance on the sovereign state, and the theory of justice that gives it shape, has led to an equivocal legacy that can be tailored to radically different agendas. Second, the already complex shape and meaning of his international reform project cannot ultimately be interpreted on neutral ideological territory. Quite simply, internationalists create markedly different Kantian legacies according to the varying ethico-political visions they hold.

WHAT IS LIBERAL INTERNATIONALISM?

Liberal internationalism is by no means a clear category. The political, ideological, and historic relationships between liberalism and politics beyond the sovereign state create not a monolithic and unchanging tradition, but disagreement and tension within its internationalist form. In this section I argue that liberal internationalism is a multifarious project of global reform, one that is characterized by historically contingent and divergent perceptions of the nature of sovereign states and the kind of freedom these agents can plausibly afford the individual both within and across territorial boundaries.

As Doyle notes, "There is no canonical description of liberalism."[4] Most agree, however, that several related political commitments give it some coherence. These commitments are clustered around the preeminent goal of individual freedom but include justice, equality, progress, the rule of law, political participation, and peace.[5] The lack of a liberal canon is the result of profound disagreement among liberals on the connotations of these core concepts in addition to the proper configuration or priority of them. Thus the freedom ideal has varied historically among liberals and the national contexts in which they have sought political reform.[6] Additionally, various liberal notions of equality, from formal equality under the law to equality of opportunity and of outcome, are the grounds for systematic limitations on individual freedom that liberals have entertained in order to construct a coherent political position. Thus a so-called liberal orientation to political society and the institutions of the state has not produced a uniformly programmatic ideology, but rather a range of alternative conceptions about how best to define and promote such values.

Liberalism is historically bound up with the coterminous rise of the modern state and the desire by certain social classes for freedom from the constraints of feudalism. The development of increasingly powerful, consolidated, and centralized states posed an immediate dilemma to the realization of freedom, one that is familiar from the above analysis of Kant. If the constraints of the feudal order were to be dismantled properly in favor of individual self-determination, then another, more rational and legitimate constraining device was to be found in the modern sovereign state. Without such a device, one individual's freedom could be purchased only at the expense of another's in the "state of nature." Certainly the sovereignty claimed by states could in principle provide a superior political-legal framework to secure individual freedom from the coercion of others—and thereby produce a rough form of justice. But the sovereign state could also impose arbitrary and intolerable ends on the very same individuals, thus negating liberty altogether and undermining the pursuit of justice within society.

In part a reaction to Hobbes's philosophy of the state and society, philosophers retrospectively judged as liberals, from Locke to the present, have sought ways around this dilemma of state sovereignty's potentially negative effects on the goal of freedom. Liberal political philosophy is largely preoccupied with how to ensure that individuals consent to or—in more positive formulations—create a system of justice and binding laws under which they, *and* the sovereign, are bound. Here the various liberal answers to this sovereignty/freedom dilemma across time are widely recognized and debated and arguably constitute the most elemental problems of political science.

The sovereignty/freedom dilemma has formed a basic part of the liberal internationalist tradition too. Quite simply, many liberals have viewed war as a state-sponsored impediment to individual freedom because it imposes high (material and other) costs on citizens—the highest of which is life itself. In this context, the internationalized version of liberalism's sovereignty/freedom dilemma concerns whether the state (and, collectively, the state system) is capable of (self)-reform toward the goal of promoting and protecting individual freedom. If the state of nature once precluded freedom domestically, and if a properly constituted sovereign state solved this within society, liberals have naturally sought ways to "domesticate" international anarchy. That is, liberalism has logically led to some internationalist vision of reform.

Fred Halliday writes that "[l]ike many concepts in social science and political theory, internationalism permits no simple, generally applicable definition."[7] But he enumerates three shared beliefs of internationalists: (1) that an "objective process," viz., the "internationalization of the world," is occurring through economic, communications, and other technological advances; (2) that such processes transform the nature of politics because actors, both state and nonstate, are responding to them; and finally, (3) that these processes are ultimately *good* because they promote "understanding, prosperity, freedom, tolerance or whatever the particular [internationalist] advocate holds dear."[8] Thus Halliday separates a *process* of internationalization from the *ends* to which its various champions aspire, suggesting that liberalism is not synonymous with internationalism.[9] Be that as it may, Halliday contends rightly that internationalism is the conviction that certain, in this case liberal, ethico-political ends cannot be restricted to any one particular society or state:

> The thought [is] that there is an international interest beyond that of nations, and that these objective changes [of internationalization] make it easier to promote.... If states are not actually rejected as ineffective or necessarily undesirable, both their effectiveness and legitimacy [are] seen as conditional to a considerable extent on this international interest.[10]

But rather than viewing reform as something that is achieved by the "objective" processes of internationalization (or globalization for that matter), most liberals have conceived of the necessity and realization of such reform on the basis of their understanding of the domestic political experience. Liberal internationalists have consistently employed, to use Suganami's phrase, a "domestic analogy" to formulate and justify international reform.[11] Historically, as Hoffmann points out, although "[t]he international dimension of liberalism was never an afterthought ... [it was also] little more than the projection of domestic liberalism worldwide."[12] But differences among liberal visions of domestic reform abound and thus we should not be surprised to find them salient among internationalists.

The differences among liberal internationalists converge on the question that Halliday mentions above: whether sovereign states are viewed as effective, desirable agents in this process of reform or as impediments that must be radically transformed if not transcended. The difficulty with many attempts to define liberal internationalism is the assumption of one, unchanging answer to this question. Such differences have been obscured by caricature in the International Relations literature, not least because of E. H. Carr's influential polemic against the liberal "utopians" of the interwar period.[13] Carr criticized liberal internationalists of the period not simply for naiveté but also for upholding an excessively formal status quo that served particular class and national (rather than universal) interests. But the irony of Carr's place in the discipline is that he glossed over several important political divisions among liberals in order to argue that they did the same.

The differences among liberal internationalists explained in the ensuing analysis do not actually constitute a debate *per se*. Rather, various liberal-minded scholars have, when they have recognized such differences, constructed a debate among thinkers across time. In such rival constructions of this tradition, many philosophers have been judged retrospectively as being liberal internationalist despite the fact that they would not recognize or identify with the term. Thinkers from John Locke, Adam Smith, and Kant to those espousing the disciplinary paradigms of the present are all placed within this political standpoint because they are held to endorse liberal reform of the unacceptable status quo of *realpolitik* and unmitigated anarchy.

MECHANISMS OF LIBERAL INTERNATIONAL REFORM

The common vision of reforming the status quo of international politics masks several differences among liberal internationalists. When these differences are acknowledged to exist, they are normally conceived to be merely mechanical or technical. What this means is that liberal internationalism is held to be concerned primarily with the issue of *how* to produce necessary changes. The domestic analogy is crucial to understanding the divisions here among internationalists because the competing liberal instruments with which to pursue individual freedom within the state have been, as Stanley Hoffmann claims, projected outward as mechanisms for reforming the international realm. Indeed, a distinctive "problem-solving" bias characterizes most depictions of what this position consists of.[14] Kjell Goldmann, for example, states that liberal internationalism is basically a project "to make international relations less conflictual by such attractive means as international institution building and cooperation."[15] It is also the promise that "international peace and security benefit if international institutions are strengthened and cooperative ties multiply across borders. International law and organization as well as economic exchanges and other forms of communication will make war an increasingly unlikely occurrence."[16]

This pragmatic and instrumental description of liberal internationalism is common in the mainstream International Relations literature.[17] However, it is both incomplete and ahistorical. It is incomplete because, in restricting liberal internationalism to a set of recipes on how to reform interstate politics, deeper ethico-political questions are ignored—or, what is more likely, their answers are merely assumed. The ethical question of why reform is justified and necessary, and the ontological question of what the international status quo consists of lie behind received convictions and conventions about how liberal internationalists should operate. It is misleading to assume, as does Goldmann, that one can discuss the different mechanisms for reform without at some point making assumptions about the different conceptions that liberals have held about the ethics of reform.[18] Indeed, as I claim below, debate on so-called liberal mechanisms of reform is implicitly animated by these more foundational assumptions. It is equally problematic to discuss the mechanisms of reform in a way that denies their historical specificity. The reason alternative mechanisms to transform international politics arise is the perception by liberals of differing contexts that the previous orthodoxies are inadequate and in need of revision. The wide variety of answers to the question of how to reform international politics thus exposes the complex historical and ideological development of liberalism within an era in which the state system emerged from the early seventeenth century.

There is a long history in Western political thought of plans for perpetual peace that anticipate a liberal internationalist concern with reform. Thinkers such as Émeric Crucé, Abbé de Saint-Pierre, and William Penn, among others, are well-known early advocates of international organization.[19] Although not "liberal" in an ideological sense, such thinkers left a coherent legacy of planning institutions of law and dispute settlement to regulate relations among states. Eventually, liberals such as Locke and Jeremy Bentham adopted the view that such institutions could function to secure more peaceful international politics by taming the uncertainty that prevailed among sovereign states. Unlike "preliberal" proponents of international organization, these thinkers relied upon their peculiarly liberal understandings of domestic society to frame prescriptions for international reform. For example, Locke claims that the "inconveniences" of prepolitical life drive individuals into political society.[20] The lack of stable (property) relations creates conflict in a generally peaceable state of nature. When individuals enter into a social contract, they do so only if the form of sovereignty functions to secure their natural rights within a prudent and stable institutional framework. Individual misperception, fear, and insecurity are allayed by a democratically representative politics within the state, albeit one of restricted suffrage. Locke applies this view of domestic politics to his prescriptions for interstate relations. For him, an international society of states is not necessarily a "state of war" (as it is for Kant) if only the norms and institutions can be established to remove misunderstanding and poor judgment on the part of states—both of which are caused by the nuisances of a poorly consolidated international society. Bentham, too, stresses the importance of "personal decision and moral judgment" by state leaders, thus drawing "closely on the effects of human nature."[21] International reform is achieved by the gradual removal of any inconveniences that may hamper state actors from perceiving correctly what is in conformity with natural rights (Locke) or calculations of the greatest good (Bentham). However, the difficulty with any plan to reform interstate relations by the mere addition of international organizations and law is that such instruments lack enforcement powers and authority. Thus, despite the implicit use of a domestic analogy, international politics is only tenuously pacified in these liberal plans rather than actually domesticated.

Hinsley writes that "[a]fter the beginning of the eighteenth century it remained possible—if unusual—for men to suggest that international peace might be obtained by means other than international organization."[22] Liberals, too, have attempted to go beyond mere international organization. For example, Adam Smith, Bentham, Richard Cobden, and John Stuart Mill believed free trade and global commerce to be as important as international organization. As Doyle notes, there is a strong history of "commercial pacifism" within liberal internationalism, which holds that "market societies are fundamentally against war."[23] Free trade and the dispersion of wealth and welfare across artificial state boundaries create interstate peace. The rejection of mercantilism and the strict limitation on governmental interference in private, entrepreneurial interests restrict those sovereign states that would otherwise impose their own conflicts upon individuals and impede the general pursuit of happiness.[24] From this perspective, the internationalization of market society not only pacifies interstate relations, it also transforms and liberates domestic societies by checking the illiberal sovereigns who resist the reform of both spheres (or by making sovereigns recalculate the best way to maintain legitimacy). This liberal mechanism is viewed as superior to international organizations alone because reform is not merely left to the constructive interventions of visionary statesmen, but is instead a "structured outcome of capitalist democracy."[25]

Subsequent liberals have been more skeptical not only of leaving international reform to the discretion of beneficent individual sovereigns, but also of the idea of rationally motivated capitalist exchange. This is because neither of these mechanisms can bind or obligate states to transcend the anarchy that exists among states that are not, by their very internal structures, peaceseeking. In this view, the constitutions of states have a profound effect upon the nature of their interrelations. It is here that Kant and Woodrow Wilson are most frequently cited to support the idea that the supreme liberal internationalist mechanism is the democratic, self-determining state. If the actual decision of whether to engage the state in war against other states is not located in "the people," meaningful international reform is impossible. International organizations can function only if comprised of self-determining peoples who are allowed to flourish.[26] International politics is thus domesticated by the principle of popular sovereignty, wherein the people have no real interest in war. (The revival of this mechanism of liberal internationalist reform after the Cold War is the focus of chapter 6.)

Many contemporary accounts of the differing historical mechanisms of liberal reform essentially stop with, and recycle, the Wilsonianism of the early twentieth century. In so doing, the tendency has been to demonstrate merely how each of the above ways of reform have been modified and refitted to the post-1945 world of international organizations, both political and economic.[27] Or, more recently, the essential validity of the liberal internationalist view has been seen to have had a very gradual, if seemingly delayed, triumph in the post-Cold War order.[28] After the decolonization process and the "third wave" of (re)democratization in the 1980s, the spread of popular sovereignty is interpreted as having come to prevail in, and to pacify, the world. In other words, when it comes to describing the range of liberal mechanisms for international reform, most mainstream, state-centric commentators restrict their analyses to those mechanisms of reform first initiated in the eighteenth and nineteenth centuries. However, such accounts are incomplete because they overlook the emergence of an entirely different strand of nonstatist liberal mechanisms of reform proposed in the twentieth century.

David Long, among others, has analyzed the important, although less influential, tradition of "new" (or radical) liberal internationalist theory. Long points out that although there are several ways to divide liberal thought, an important split is between classical and "new" liberalism. This terminology is adapted from Michael Freeden's work on the evolution of British liberalism.[29] Freeden claims that as liberal ideology developed, it cleaved because its initially laissez-faire character became viewed as merely protecting the vested interests of certain sections of political society. The radical thrust of liberalism, as the pursuit of universal freedom and the challenging of privilege, was silenced by classical liberal defenses of such privilege. In response, new liberals such as L. T. Hobhouse, J. A. Hobson, and John Maynard Keynes advocated a greater role for the state and a positive conception of individual freedom to promote liberal ethico-political goals.[30] Long applies this analysis to internationalism, claiming a similar split among liberals over the question of how to reform international politics. The previous liberal answers to this question that have been discussed, i.e., free trade, international law, and national self-determination, are similar to the extent that they embrace a laissez-faire stance toward the economy in addition to international organization. This classical liberal stance was judged by new liberals as being too formal in that it optimistically overlooked the material requirements for peaceful change and was state-centric. Classical liberal internationalism assumes that meaningful and lasting reform occurs when it is directed by the will of the state and states in concert (albeit states constrained by the "invisible hand" of market forces or popular sovereignty).

As Michael Joseph Smith notes, however, "The liberal tradition has also served to ground dissent from a perceived statist bias among most international leaders. In these terms, the tradition remains alive and vital."[31] The emergence of such dissent within liberalism is a result of skepticism of the classical mechanisms of reform, especially in historical periods of crisis— the most salient of which was the "shattered" confidence in liberalism as a result of the First World War.[32] In the aftermath, the territorial state became viewed by many new liberals as just too recalcitrant and obstinate an agent to lead reform of the increasingly destructive consequences of anarchy. It is thus unsurprising that in the past century there arose newer varieties of internationalism such as David Mitrany's functionalist approach.[33] His position, and the subsequent neofunctionalist reformulation,[34] downplay the importance of formal interstate mechanisms and legal-institutional frameworks in favor of transnational associations of legitimacy that alter human loyalties to particular states.[35] For this reason, as Charles Pentland notes, functionalism views reform as occurring "not through, above or beyond, but *despite* the nation-state."[36] The contested question of how liberal internationalist reform is to be carried out has thus been enlarged to include a deep pessimism in the capacity of sovereign states, even though the majority of mainstream liberal descriptions of this tradition will ignore its political and ethical importance.[37]

Underneath such divisions among liberals about how to reform international politics there lingers a deeper, unresolved issue. What is ultimately at stake in the various prescriptions regarding the mechanisms of reform are the *ends* shared necessarily by all truly liberal strains of international thought. Does the sovereign state enable or impede the overarching goal of freedom and, moreover, a freedom that is realized justly? This recalls Halliday's claim that in internationalism generally, the legitimacy of the state is dependent upon a transcendent ideological goal. For liberals, then, the question of mechanisms is ultimately subordinate to an ethical standard or justification.

Some liberals are much more optimistic and confident about the ethical capacities of the state—they envisage the limitation and reform of its sovereignty through constitutionally mandated individual rights. If a state transgresses the established conception of individual freedom, it is no longer truly "sovereign" because it has violated the popular will upon which it must be based. In such a case, rebellion and revolution have been justified.[38] State sovereignty is considered to be largely compatible with individual freedom insofar as it is constituted and legitimated correctly, i.e., with some view of its just organization. But does this type of liberal optimism about sovereignty pertain in the international context? As argued above, liberals such as Locke, Bentham, and Kant hold that institutional reform can occur successfully among sovereign states. The possibility of individual freedom *through* the agency of state sovereignty is affirmed when states are viewed as capable of transforming their internal constitutions and, as a result, the conflictual relations among them. International law and organizations serve a quasi-constitutional function in mediating the external and internal sovereignty of states, acting as a surrogate world government.[39] This predominant vision of liberal reform is, as Hoffmann has generalized about the entire tradition, essentially about "performing ... negative tasks."[40] Individual freedom is ultimately promoted by the coordinated effort of states to *refrain* from intervening in each other's political affairs; and the ethico-political bias of this particular vision is stated clearly by Doyle:

> The basic postulate of liberal international theory holds that states have the right to be free from foreign intervention. Since morally autonomous

citizens hold rights to liberty, the states that democratically represent them
have the right to exercise political independence. Mutual respect for these
rights becomes the touchstone of international liberal theory.[41]

But Doyle's statement is too sweeping because there are other stances
within the development of liberal internationalism that are much more
ambivalent, if not outright skeptical, about the compatibility of sovereignty and freedom.

For one thing, a much deeper distrust of sovereignty has emerged from
liberals who claim that it is precisely *because* of the international context
that states are not adequate to the task of self-reform and cannot therefore
function to secure individual freedom. Kant's texts can be rightly invoked
here because (as I claimed in chapter 3) he views interstate anarchy to
be too hostile an environment for states to *purposefully* reform their
relations. Sovereigns—and particularly nonrepublican ones—are likely to
make exceptions for themselves from any peace arrangements reached,
and therefore other states would necessarily have to engage in strategic
action in self-defense.[42] Kant's teleological "guarantee" of international
reform clearly implies the insufficiency of sovereign states, even ones that
are based on a large measure of domestic justice, to fulfill the requirements of individual freedom. For mere interstate anarchy can cause the
imposition of wars upon individuals of any state.[43] The fact that Kant
requires a philosophy of history to envisage possible reform should be
viewed as a consequence of a problematic application by Kant of his theory of justice to international politics. This is because Kant rejects a global
sovereign required by his own formal principles of justice; his nonideal
vision of reform allows anarchy to continue undomesticated. As argued
above, it is only the worst *effects* of anarchy that Kant hopes will be
pacified in time.

Nevertheless, Kant's skepticism of the capacity of sovereign states to
accomplish self-reform anticipates the antistatist temper of many twentieth-
century liberals. Liberal optimism in the state, and any residual Kantian
faith in historical teleology, for that matter, was challenged by crisis events
that seemingly demonstrated that the classical internationalist mechanisms
of reform were unable to prevent major wars. As Richardson notes, international organizations in particular were viewed in less sympathetic terms:
"[T]he idea that [such mechanisms] ... might become a bulwark of privilege, a way of preserving the established order by other means, was
expressed in the interwar period by the dissatisfied, 'revisionist' powers, and
critics of liberalism such as E. H. Carr were quick to challenge the moral
pretensions of the powers upholding the League of Nations."[44] But this
classical liberal internationalist vision of international organizations—as

merely the playthings of powerful states—became the theme of poststatist
liberals such as David Mitrany.[45] Moreover, the rise of nationalism made
the idea of popular sovereignty far more problematic than classical internationalists had assumed. As Hoffmann states, "[s]elf-determination was
seen as the necessary corollary of liberal self-government, and it was this
conviction that reshaped the vision of final international harmony into
a vision of nation-states with liberal regimes: Wilson's dream."[46] And after
the horrors of national autonomy were demonstrated in world wars,
many "liberals have moved from regarding nationalism as a liberating
doctrine compatible with the goals of limiting state power and pacifying
international competition to a recognition that unbridled nationalism has
proven in the modern era to be one of the strongest ideological weapons
in the armory of independent sovereign states."[47] For these reasons,
the classical liberal hope for individual freedom through state sovereignty
is no longer entirely hegemonic in the tradition. And the notion that
liberals cannot rely (exclusively) upon the ethical capabilities of sovereign
states signals the need if not possibility of cosmopolitical solutions to
international injustice and the requirements of individual autonomy.

It is in this divided context that Kant's ambiguous place within the
liberal internationalist tradition is best explained. This is because, within
Kant's thought the entire "international problem" is, as I argued above,
considered from a perspective of overriding concern for individual freedom in a phenomenal world populated by sovereign states. In other words,
Kant's reform project is an answer—one that is, as we have seen, highly
complex—to an ethical question of sovereignty's relationship to the goals
of freedom and justice. It transpires that his problematic stance on the
ethics of reform has been invoked by contemporary internationalists to
support two distinct and rival visions of reform, one statist and the other
poststatist. However, as I argue below, even when the ethical moorings
of Kant's international project are taken more seriously, it is the ambiguity of his own theory of justice that has led to rival accounts of the nature
of reform.

CONTEMPORARY LIBERAL INTERNATIONALISM
THROUGH KANT'S "LEGACY"

How does Kant's legacy support, sustain, and even challenge a subsequent
tradition of liberal internationalism? His texts predate and anticipate
liberalism, and as a result there is a large measure of ambiguity concerning whether and how his political philosophy supports the liberal quest to
both justify and reform the political structures, processes, and institutions

that have developed since the late eighteenth century. Kant's stance on the sovereign state and theory of justice create an ambiguous intellectual and ideological legacy for liberalism and its internationalist form.

There are many compelling reasons why liberal internationalism enjoyed a renaissance after the Cold War. What is less obvious are the reasons why Kant has been singled out as a key foundation for the reassertion of progressive reform of international politics. A sudden ubiquity of Kant as a foundational source of liberal international theory is perfectly plausible and, simultaneously, quite remarkable. It is understandable because he is perhaps the only intellectual forerunner to liberal internationalism who can, superficially at least, be used to lend support to any and nearly all of the different mechanisms of reform described above. There is evidence in Kant of an economic liberalism given his view that war is entirely incompatible with the "spirit of commerce."[48] There is even more ample and convincing evidence of Kant's support for a League of Nations, international law, and the pacific effects of the right type of constitution.[49] And, as I argue below, Kant's philosophy plausibly supports an increasingly poststatist, cosmopolitical world order in which pacifying forms of political representation are not tied exclusively to territorial statehood.[50] Taking Kant's statements on the mechanisms of international reform out of context—that is, detached from his larger justification of sovereignty and theory of justice—is highly problematic. It leads to the anachronistic impression that Kant has the same assumptions, concerns, and agenda as do subsequent and modern liberals simply because he anticipated these tools of political reform. But the use of Kant's legacy to speak of the ethics of reform is also remarkable and surprising. This is because the underlying foundations of his political theory are basically at odds with the predominant Anglo-American versions of political liberalism. As noted above, the absolute autonomy of morals and the priority of formal over material causes that it engenders within his theory of justice ground a peculiar form of liberalism—one that has, as I have explored in previous chapters, several illiberal facets, especially when it comes to the sovereign state. Jens Bartelson similarly notes that the majority of contemporary internationalist references to Kant "neglect or distort some of his ideas by overlooking the foundations of his political philosophy, and instead merely reiterate ... the problems that Kant himself sought to solve."[51] Ignorance of Kant's critical philosophy perhaps justifies R. B. J. Walker's harsh comment that it is only a "kitsch Kantianism" that underlies contemporary theorizing in International Relations.[52] The freedom/sovereignty dilemma identified above and the Kantian quest for justice explains not merely the peculiarities of his international reform project, but also his ideological absorption into contemporary liberal internationalism.

Recent International Relations scholarship is also divided on the issue of whether the sovereign state is adequate to promoting and providing for individual freedom and whether it can produce international justice. Since the early 1980s, Michael Doyle and Andrew Linklater have published contrasting views on the ethical nature of internationalism. The differences between them illustrate that Kant's inclusion into a contemporary discourse has not provided an unambiguous legacy. Doyle and Linklater are significant because their interpretations of Kant have been influential in the field, spurring different Kantian "legacies." In each of their accounts, Kant's legacy is one that supports contrasting views of the sovereign state's essential compatibility with freedom. But Doyle and Linklater implicitly appeal to different elements of Kant's ambiguous vision of sovereignty and the theory of justice from which it is drawn. By making their assumptions more explicit, a substantial debate within the liberal tradition and its future relevance is, I think, clarified.

The most dominant Kantian "legacy" in the discipline is initiated by Doyle. His seminal 1983 two-part article on Kant and liberalism has the virtue of giving both a philosophical and a social scientific explanation of what is, according to at least one observer, "as close as anything we have to an empirical law in international relations."[53] The "law" in question is the absence of major wars among liberal states since the early nineteenth century. Doyle claims there is a philosophical explanation in Kant's writings for two different liberal legacies: first, the increased mitigation of anarchy among liberal sovereign states; and, second, the persistent reality of liberal aggression if not simply hostility toward illiberal forms of sovereignty. Doyle identifies the democratic sovereign state as the most important cause for both liberal legacies. In keeping with classical forms of liberal internationalism, an equal balancing of individual freedom within such states has the external effect argued by Kant: These states are more likely to coordinate their wills and act on basic principles of international justice: i.e., coexistence and noninterference. However, the absence of this coordinating mechanism between the "inside" and the "outside," between liberal and illiberal regimes, not only permits anarchy to reign but prompts wars of missionary liberalization by liberal states wishing to domesticate international politics.[54] (A more detailed analysis and critique of Doyle's basic thesis about the relationship between democracy and peace is the subject of chapter 6.) What is of interest here is the specific way in which Doyle constructs a legacy out of the ambiguous materials that are available from Kant's texts. Two related points are of significance in Doyle's depiction of the Kantian legacy. First, because state sovereignty—at least in its liberal form—is the crucial mechanism of international reform, its existence is a given necessity. Second, the internationalist agenda as specified by this interpretation of Kant has already been largely achieved by "actually existing" liberal regimes;[55] the only remaining task is the continued mitigation of anarchy through the elaboration of extant principles of liberal sovereignty. Doyle certainly acknowledges that there are social and political problems unresolved in liberal states. Moreover, he is concerned with explaining the more limited outcome of interstate peace rather than freedom. Nonetheless, in truncating Kant's vision, Doyle implicitly attributes to Kant the view that individual liberty is compatible with whatever existing amount of self-reform liberal sovereign states are capable of. Thus, state sovereignty is in principle fully compatible with individual freedom, and it is the foundation of international justice.

At roughly the same time Doyle published his statist reading of Kant's "legacy," Linklater's book, *Men and Citizens in the Theory of International Relations,* appeared. Linklater does not wish merely to vindicate classical liberal internationalism but to question its traditionally state-centric assumptions as regards the means to the end of universal emancipation. In this and subsequent publications, Linklater relies upon the notion of "critique" to illustrate the historical possibility of progressive change in international relations.[56] He proposes that "an alternative framework with which to defend the internationalist" project is "exemplified" by Kant's legacy.[57] Human freedom can be satisfied only if we follow Kant's philosophical example and become aware "of the possibility of human intervention in the social world in order to modify its nature."[58] It is on this basis that Linklater claims that the Kantian legacy supports "a radical transformation of the political world in the direction of that condition in which all human beings live in conformity with the imperatives grounded within their rational natures."[59] Linklater certainly realizes that Kant places a high premium on the limited moral improvement of individuals within the framework of the state.[60] However, because sovereign states are morally subordinate to individual autonomy, they cannot be counted upon as the sole "trustees" of international reform.[61] Kant's philosophy, as elaborated by Linklater, appears to anticipate a postsovereign world order.[62] He is thus skeptical that existing republican sovereign states are sufficient to enable human autonomy—even within Kant's thought.[63] Linklater's Kantian legacy is an internationalism in which the demand of sovereignty as a political device for ethical ends is eventually eclipsed because of its ultimately detrimental relationship to human freedom. This line of analysis, while less influential in mainstream scholarship than Doyle's, has nonetheless influenced the discipline.

Why are these two such fundamentally contrasting explications of Kant's legacy possible? One credible answer is suggested by Jens Bartelson;

namely, that paradoxical and contradictory depictions of Kant among modern International Relations scholars result predictably from the foundational Kantian dualism: "[W]hat accounts for their contradictory character is the fact that, although they start out by accepting the distinction between the concepts of nature and freedom" in the *Critique of Pure Reason*, "they all conclude by giving the one concept a more privileged position than the other in their readings of his philosophy of politics."[64] When *nature* is given priority, perpetual peace is a rational chimera motivating only modest reform among robustly sovereign states; but when *freedom* is given more weight, perpetual peace and the so-called kingdom of ends are real goals for which to strive and achieve in history. Bartelson does not consider Doyle and Linklater in his analysis but his assessment appears relevant. The Doyle and Linklater conceptions of Kant's legacy are to an extent one-sided because they privilege one of two radically distinct existential poles between which Kant places humans. When either nature or freedom is prioritized within Kant's system, the solution to international anarchy rests on two substantially different ethico-political visions. As a result, the Kantian legacy becomes divided and contested as a basis for the contemporary internationalist agenda.

However, Bartelson's explanation of the divergent conceptions of Kant's intellectual legacy is too general because it considers this problem of interpretation from the most abstract vantage point—metaphysics. Thus, although Doyle's classical statist internationalism gravitates closer to natural necessity than does Linklater's poststatism, such an explanation is not specific enough. It is necessary to go beyond the nature/freedom dualism itself and to explain, as I have done in the above chapters, how this underlying chasm animates Kant's position on sovereignty and justice. From this vantage point, we see that Doyle and Linklater rely on implicit understandings of the relationship between sovereignty and freedom in Kant's political theory. While Doyle takes the goal of freedom to be a serious end of liberal internationalism, he absorbs the *formalism* of Kant's theory of justice. His position is more consistent with the "conservative" interpretive stance identified at the end of chapter 2. Freedom is thus merely a regulative ideal, a symbolic device that is perpetually restricted in its application to the material world of politics. As a result, the phenomenally existing sovereign state—albeit one that is republican—is sufficient for external individual freedom and thus effectively terminates the nature of international reform. Such reform consists merely of the continued diffusion of republican forms of sovereignty. By contrast, Linklater's reading of Kant's internationalism clearly takes up the more radical interpretation to which I alluded at the end of chapter 2. The cosmopolitan kingdom of ends of Kant's moral philosophy is viewed as a real goal that cannot be met merely through the agency of the (republican) sovereign state. Moreover, the division of humanity into exclusive territorial spheres governed by sovereign agents is of only transient significance to the realization of this moral goal. International justice for Linklater would thus seem to draw more upon Kant's second justification of international reform, the *material* one that places individual autonomy at the center of transformation. As a result, Linklater drops Kant's robust (if not dogmatic) justification of sovereignty and embraces the possibility of alternative political frameworks for the promotion of individual autonomy.

CONCLUSION

In this chapter I have explored the profound differences among historical and contemporary liberals over the mechanics and ethics of reform. These differences have been explained in relation to the ambiguous legacy that Kant has left for subsequent reformers of international anarchy. Given the dualistic nature of his theory of justice, I have argued that his status as a foundational source of internationalism is understandably divided between competing statist and poststatist legacies, both of which presume that the sovereign state has a particular relationship to the ethical goals of individual freedom and international justice. In the following two chapters I explain how such ethico-political divisions within liberal internationalism have driven markedly different agendas in the realm of international institutionalization and the role of democracy in political reform.

CHAPTER 5

THE CRISIS OF LIBERAL INTERNATIONALISM: FROM INTERNATIONAL TO GLOBAL GOVERNING INSTITUTIONS

It is not only the order of Yalta (bipolarity and the Cold War) and the order of Versailles (the borders and states that emerged from the Austro-Hungarian empires) that are being challenged. The order of Westphalia—the idea of a system based on territoriality and the sovereignty of states—is also being called into question.

—Pierre Hassner[1]

As Stanley Hoffmann has claimed, liberal internationalism appears to confront a host of political, intellectual and moral crises at exactly the time when its victory seemed at hand—the post-Cold War era.[2] The aim in this chapter is to give an alternative account of the significance of such a crisis. I argue that liberal internationalism's "failings and limitations," to use Hoffmann's phrase, are rooted in the inability of sovereign states and statist intergovernmental institutions to meet the growing demands for global justice. In an era of rapid globalization and change, the excessively formal and state-centric conception of world order that orients today's international institutions is problematic. This conception of order is premised mainly on a classical liberal internationalist understanding of justice among states; however, it is one that is unable to address effectively the demands for autonomy and rights made by individuals and groups globally. Consequently, the central goals of liberalism are unmet in today's world order in part because of the constraints that classical liberal internationalist ideals impose on peaceful change in an era of globalization.

The crisis of liberal internationalism is best addressed by liberals who aspire to make international institutions more relevant and more open to the demands made by the world's marginalized, rather than simply by the world's privileged and powerful, actors. In this chapter I argue that this requires a change in how liberals view justice and international organization, one that goes beyond the classical liberal stance of thinkers such as Kant. This would mean encouraging a transformation in international institutions to make them more cosmopolitan in terms of the interests they serve, in addition to making them more open to the demands placed upon them by nonstate actors in global civil society. Kant and his competing legacies analyzed in the preceding chapters guide my assessment in this chapter of contemporary trends in the theory and practice of governance. The tensions and paradoxes that animate Kant's influence on liberalism are relevant to explaining the dominant ideological and normative parameters of international governance. If liberal internationalism is to be reconstructed to make it more relevant, it will require liberals to take up the radical potential of Kantian enlightenment discussed at the end of chapter 2. That is, rather than reinforcing only the "top down" vision of state-led reform found in classical liberal internationalism, it is more promising to envisage a radical internationalism that is open to the material conditions of human autonomy.

The first section of this chapter explores and puts in critical context Hoffmann's claim that liberal internationalism is in crisis. I claim that although he is correct to emphasize the threats to liberal ethico-political commitments posed by state fragmentation and economic globalization, the solution to these problems does not lie simply in reinforcing statist intergovernmental structures and practices. When viewed from a longer-term perspective, liberal internationalism has always been in crisis when its ethical promise of justice has been constrained by status quo–oriented institutions and authoritative practices.

The second section takes up E. H. Carr's historically specific and critical analysis of liberal internationalism and applies it to the present. Carr's pertinent lesson is that the liberal goal of justice is effectively undermined and subverted when the dominant institutional order is too closed to the demands of actors whose interests are marginalized by the formal rules of that order. I then elaborate and extend Carr's critique of liberal internationalism by comparing two models of governance, one that is statist and the other poststatist. Using examples from recent international theory and events, I claim that the formalistic and statist liberal bias of the former model actually sustains and will likely aggravate the crisis of liberal internationalism. Efforts to develop a poststatist account of global institutionalization hold out the promise of addressing the crisis noted by Carr as early as the 1930s and rearticulated by Hoffmann in the 1990s.

THE CRISIS OF LIBERAL INTERNATIONALISM

In March 1999 the North Atlantic Treaty Organization launched a war against Yugoslavia to curb the abuse of human rights in its Kosovo province. This was done, however, without the approval of the UN Security Council. While many states, including Russia, China, and, of course, the regime in Belgrade, viewed this as an unjust violation of a sovereign state's territorial integrity—in addition to the UN's formal norms—NATO's leaders justified their actions as a rightful protection of the Albanian Kosovars.[3] In this polarized context, the victims of the massacres, revenge killings, rapes, lootings, and expulsions tended to collectively assess the rightfulness of NATO's actions in terms of whether this organization would or could effectively promote their basic rights and entitlements. The fact that NATO has arguably not succeeded in upholding the entitlements of all Kosovars consistently leads many to suggest that its actions and current role are fundamentally unjust, however sound the original intent.[4]

In the winter and spring of 1999–2000, thousands of protesters attempted to shut down the meetings of the World Trade Organization in Seattle and of the World Bank in Washington, D.C. Protesters claimed that the central institutions of the liberalizing global economy were unjust in their failure to take the interests, welfare, and basic rights of "the people" seriously. The leaders of member states, and of these multilateral economic institutions, were quick to defend the extent to which the benefits of market liberalization and globalization could be harnessed in favor of social equity and, moreover, could be pursued in tandem with human rights and environmentalism.[5]

These events appear to signal the "crisis of liberal internationalism" that Stanley Hoffmann describes and laments in an influential 1995 *Foreign Policy* article.[6] As Hoffmann warns, the classical liberal internationalist reform tools described in the last chapter are woefully inadequate in the face of the tumultuous domestic, international, and global political upheavals we now face. The fragmentation and collapse of states as (in principle, at least) universal and impartial protectors of people's interests and rights, in addition to the inability and unwillingness of states to pursue and uphold such interests and rights in the face of intensified economic globalization, undermine the ethical goals central to liberal governance. Hoffmann also suggests that liberal internationalism's inherent contradictions are now revealed by the recent pathological growth of the free-market ideology and the ideal of national self-determination. The processes of globalization and state fragmentation have unleashed and radicalized these liberal internationalist icons at the expense of other liberal values, like the rule of law and accountability, that are upheld through democratic institutions.

Thus, the Kosovo crisis and events in Seattle and Washington, D.C., would signal, in Hoffmann's terms, the profoundly inadequate reform agenda encapsulated in classical liberal internationalism. They demonstrate that the threats to individual freedom in today's world do not simply emanate from interstate conflict. As he points out, it is not only the "Moloch of [state] power" that is the problem. It is, rather, the "chaos from below" resulting from the "disintegration of [state] power" that puts liberal goals in jeopardy and crisis. Thus, "What is now at stake is the very nature of the state. The Westphalian system that has inspired all theories of international relations presupposed well-determined states, clashing or cooperating."[7] But the Westphalian order has been challenged by recent historical experience.

Indeed, the problem for liberal internationalism as it has been conventionally framed—that is, the promotion of peace among states—may not be that it has yet to succeed, but that it has largely done so already.[8] Anarchy has been domesticated in that states are increasingly tamed by popular sovereignty and have, moreover, ceded crucial powers to the global market economy. Thus the traditional liberal internationalist ontology of a "state of nature" populated by dangerously autonomous states, standing like titans against each other, is no longer an accurate or useful depiction of contemporary politics. As Jef Huysmans notes, the processes of globalization flow perfectly from liberalism's premises: "The very liberal value of freedom ... [sustains] the unconstrained movement of goods, services, capital and people." On the other hand, however, the "intensification of [such] flows challenges the core elements of the liberal institutional order."[9] This institutional order is the assumed foundation of autonomous states that are able to respond to the demands of their citizens. The classical liberal internationalist idea that reform consists of domesticating sovereign states in anarchy is thus problematic in part because states have been systematically giving up autonomy in the face of market pressures. As Hoffmann states, "[M]any of the powers given up by the states have gone not to central institutions, but to the markets."[10] But the globalized market economy has "not merely, and beneficially, constrained the power of states .... It has also deprived them of some of their ability to perform necessary tasks, to carry out the basic functions liberalism never intended to remove from them."[11]

The novelty of liberal internationalism's crisis ought not be exaggerated. David Long and I have argued, for example, that liberalism and its internationalist form are always enmeshed in a crisis. An ever-present gap between this ideology's abstract, universalistic ethico-political principles and the concrete and historically particular configurations of rights, duties, and political institutions create the regular perception of crisis.[12] Moreover, this perception of crisis is held not only by critics of liberalism (such as E. H. Carr) but also by critical liberals who seek to reform and reconstruct the tradition by turning away from orthodox reform tools. Hoffmann's analysis shows, however, that today's crisis is highly conditioned by perceptions of globalization and the challenges it poses to sovereign states. State autonomy and institutions are exercised within the context of a simultaneous deterritorialization of the economy, society, and governing practices by nonsovereign actors. Consequently, states are limited agents in terms of meeting the demands for justice traditionally made on them. Globalization is propelled by a recognizably liberal (or "neo"-liberal) assault on the legitimacy of states to act politically in ways that impinge upon market freedom, as it is also recognizably liberal to decry the incapacity of states to realize the claims to justice upon which their legitimacy rests. But it is not just encroaching markets that are problematic; states have been the agents of their own delegitimation as they have failed to uphold the basic entitlements of citizens by collapsing into disorder and/or by turning against their own populations.

The recent events in Kosovo and social movement reactions to globalization thus exhibit signals that classical liberal internationalism is on troubled ground. But liberal internationalism's most recent crisis should not simply be diagnosed only to be lamented. In the rest of this chapter I explain the most fundamental reasons for this crisis in addition to suggesting changes in perspective needed in an era of globalization. Although Hoffmann is correct that a decline of state autonomy and capacity is central to this crisis, I argue that simple retrenchment to a world in which classical liberal internationalism "works," or in which state-centric assumptions could function smoothly, is unlikely and undesirable. This does not, however, mean that states are unimportant. To the contrary, as Cecelia Lynch claims, "[A] sophisticated internationalist stance cannot simply ignore the state ... it must [rather] call the state to accountability in ensuring social and economic welfare while looking to international norms to place control on statist militarism."[13] Because states are now enmeshed in (and contribute to) global economic and normative processes of transformation, there is hope for the "sophisticated" internationalism

Lynch calls for. The "accountability," "welfare," and "international norms" to which she refers are all central to the institutionalization of justice within and across existing states that have been the promises of liberal internationalism since at least Kant.

THE PROMISE OF LIBERAL INTERNATIONALISM: THE PURSUIT OF JUSTICE

International Relations as a discipline has been profoundly shaped by the perceived failure of liberal internationalism to live up to its promises. As noted in chapter 4, E. H. Carr claimed it was the dangerously wide gap between the utopian postulates of liberals and the reality of power politics among states that caused the crisis in which Europe found itself leading up to World War II. In spite of his noted tendency to ignore the diversity of interwar liberal thought, Carr's analysis contains some important, lasting criticism. In his view, liberal internationalist reform failed to keep the peace in Europe because its concepts were overly formal, abstract, and removed from the particulars of conflicting political interests and the perceptions of competing national actors.[14] Liberalism's "harmony of interests" ideology masked the reality that the prevailing world order promoted a particular set of powerful states' interests while failing to provide . openings for the less powerful to voice their demands.[15] In such a context, the requirements of peaceful change and authentic reform were subordinate to maintaining a status quo that benefited the (powerful) few.

Carr's brand of critical realism attempts to explain the failings of the League of Nations and the deep limitations of international morality and law. Typical of other realists, Carr focuses on the pursuit by state leaders of their national interests rather than simply justice.[16] He also emphasizes how a decentralized, anarchic order was inhospitable to the simple realization of universal goals.[17] But Carr does not aim to categorically undermine the typically liberal ideal of international justice, or the potential of international institutions to promote such ideals. To the contrary, he critically questioned the extraordinarily limited capacity of existing international organization to actually realize the claims to justice that its advocates espoused. Unlike other realists, then, Carr does not simply claim that anarchy will undermine international organization. Rather, he demonstrates that the legitimacy of institutions such as the League is seriously compromised by the prevailing and partial interests behind their formation.[18] Quite simply, an international organization that cannot (or will not) enforce authoritatively anything but the wishes of its most powerful members is inherently problematic and likely to fail in achieving purported goals of peace and justice.[19] Without a wider degree of recognized authority and a much greater degree of impartiality, the effective functioning of such institutions would be seriously compromised.[20]

The lesson Carr draws is particularly appropriate: that we ought to seriously question whether contemporary international organization contains sufficient, widely recognized, and inclusive mechanisms for at least dealing with (authoritatively accepting or rejecting), and thereby reconciling, the justice claims of different actors.[21] Without attention to the claims of dissatisfied states, for example, international organization could never approximate the goals its advocates have claimed possible.[22] Carr's legacy thus arguably takes us to the heart of a problem with liberal internationalism not just of his own time but that plagues today's globalizing world. Going beyond the mere skepticism of other realists, Carr suggests that the problem of liberal internationalist practice is a failure to at least recognize, if not always accommodate, the importance of claims to justice and complaints of injustice by actors—both state and nonstate—in a context that supposedly lacks a well-ordered, cohesive set of authoritative practices by which to adjudicate competing claims. Carr's critical realist analysis is thus premised on the typically internationalist notion of developing institutional mechanisms capable of what he terms "peaceful change." An essential component of such reform is international organization that is open and well suited to harnessing the demands of competing actors to have their perceived entitlements recognized and respected by others.[23] To what extent are existing liberal conceptions of international governance suited to this task, especially in the post - Cold War era that has seen changes in the capacities of sovereign states and the rising importance of nonstate actors and movements? Are the traditional liberal internationalist institutions of reform and peaceful change sufficiently open to the justice demands of political actors that are marginal to the interests of the powerful? If not, the contemporary crisis of liberal internationalism may not be all that different in substance than in Carr's time.

In the ensuing analysis I focus on the limited way in which contemporary theorists of international governance and institutionalization have—for the most part tacitly—taken up Carr's legacy in relation to the basic problem of justice. In particular, I focus on the work of two scholars, David A. Welch and Terry Nardin, as having illuminated and theorized two distinct and important features present in Carr's critical analysis of liberal internationalism: the "justice motive" and "authoritative practices." As I shall claim, however, Welch and Nardin seem to advocate an extremely formal liberalism that fails ultimately to address Carr's concern that the material and other justice claims of political agents reside outside the extant framework of international law and its statist morality. In this way,

Welch and Nardin reaffirm the classical liberal internationalism also exemplified by Kant's excessively formal theory of justice analyzed in previous chapters.

The Justice Motive versus Authoritative Practice

Welch's study of war contains findings that apply to liberal conceptions of international justice and governance. He concludes that wars are frequently ignited by perceptions of justice and injustice and not simply because—as realists assume—each state contains an "aversion to loss and an appetite for gain."[24] However, he qualifies this claim by distinguishing between (1) justice as a motive and (2) justice as an authoritative practice, grounded in the widely accepted and robust norms of international institutions. The justice motive is "*the drive to correct a perceived discrepancy between entitlements and benefits*" or "a reaction to a perceived discrepancy between entitlements and benefits."[25] Welch claims that the justice motive is something negative, a destabilizing force that must be contained and harnessed: "The justice motive ... will continue to be a part of the problem until it can become a part of the solution."[26] And this can happen only when the justice motive is channeled appropriately into the formalized practices of international institutions that can settle authoritatively disputes about entitlements. For Welch, the justice motive explains something important about the reasons (state) actors behave in certain ways and thus why they might accept or reject the legitimacy of existing international laws and institutions.[27] This explains not only why states fight and why the work of international organizations is forestalled by conflicts over rightful entitlement; it also potentially explains the opposite—why states would seek the construction of institutions that can authoritatively settle disputes about right. As we have learned about Kant and classical liberal internationalism more generally, rational actors will seek an authoritative institutional status quo to constrain others from treading upon those rights. While the justice motive is a problem, its solution is international justice as a gradually more impressive body of de facto or status quo authoritative practices.

In light of this distinction, Welch asserts that, ultimately, "Justice is a virtue of a particular type of order: namely, one which defines and protects entitlements to legitimate expectations and resolves conflicting claims through a procedure widely regarded as legitimate—what John Rawls calls a 'well-ordered society.' "[28] Welch concedes, as does Rawls of course, that the extent to which an international society can become as "well-ordered" as the domestic polity is limited especially by such factors as cultural pluralism and therefore conflicting understandings of the good life. But there is, within this more or less "anarchical society," to use Hedley Bull's phrase, a reasonably well-ordered layer of authoritative practices and international laws that can do the job.[29]

Terry Nardin's work on the question of international justice is also relevant here. He introduces an influential distinction between international society as a "purposive" and as a "practical" association of states. Nardin holds that the essence of international governance is the idea that purposes be kept out of things, and that international institutionalization be merely about the procedures that allow states with very different purposes to coexist. He sees evidence since the late eighteenth century that the theory and successful practice of traditional international law is practical rather than purposive—that is, to use Welch's language, dedicated to authoritative practices rather than satisfying every state's particular and subjective justice motive.[30] As Nardin writes, the international legal status quo constitutes a "meta-state," one that is formed by "an association of political communities united through the authority of common rules governing their relations but lacking the [purposive] institutions through which the laws of political community are ordinarily created or applied."[31] In other words, these authoritative practices create a form of governance without government.[32]

Nardin's understanding of institutions and justice exemplifies a classical liberal bias that we have noted in previous chapters. As Chris Brown writes, in this view, justice "is defined largely in formal or procedural terms; social justice is not a major focus."[33] To be fair, this does not mean that Nardin, Welch, and other such liberals are opposed to social justice, welfare assistance, or aid for poor states or individuals. It is, rather, the view that material, substantive or purposive ends do not belong in international governance. If such governance is not "limited to clarifying and strengthening the focus and procedures to be observed by states in their external relations, [and] to determining the requirements of these forms and procedures in particular situations," a destabilizing and disorderly Pandora's box will likely, as Nardin argues, be opened.[34] Such conflict is deemed all too likely because substantive purposes would negate the inherent (and desirable) cultural plurality of international society. And states are deemed by Welch and Nardin—at least in the present world order—to be the best containers of identity and regulators of diversity among peoples.

This classical liberal conceptualization of justice is highly problematic. In making the distinction between justice as a motive ("purpose," in Nardin's language) and justice as an authoritative practice (that is purely "practical" in intent), these analysts fail to strike a balance between

so-called subjective motives and positive authoritative practices. As anticipated by Carr, liberal international governance fails when its basic
institutions reject too strongly justice motives and purposes and endorse
too strongly the extant status quo. Hence the meaning of justice is too
"conservative" and closed to the justice demands of actors who perceive
themselves excluded or wronged. It is, moreover, too formal and too state-
centric in an era of globalization.

STATIST AND POSTSTATIST GOVERNANCE

In this section I situate the more classical liberal assumptions of thinkers
like Welch and Nardin within a "statist" model of international governance. I then juxtapose this model with a "poststatist" model of global
governance that emphasizes the pursuit of justice within globalization. To
illustrate some of the differences between each model, I refer to the "crisis" events mentioned above, that is, the recent reaction by social movements to global economic liberalization and the events in Kosovo in 1999.

Welch and Nardin view the key tenets of international justice as having
a universal scope with applicability to all sovereign states on the globe's
surface. They are interested in how to sustain and govern just interstate
relations in a decentralized world order. As Nardin writes, when appropriately conceived, just international institutions will govern political
relations among states without the legislative mechanisms with which we
are accustomed in states. He states that "[t]he history of international relations since 1815 is ... in part a series of experiments in international
government."[35] Welch similarly refers to the extant patchwork of regimes,
legal norms, and international authoritative practices as sufficient to produce a kind of governance without government.[36] Welch and Nardin are
not ignorant of transnational forces and the growing interdependence
of states and societies; they also do not deny the existence of nonsovereign
actors, although they certainly do not take pains to give a theoretical
account of them. Quite simply, these facts do not override the normative
centrality of the state—they both approvingly cite Hedley Bull's view that
states are a "positive" and hopefully enduring element of world order.[37] As
Welch claims, "the actors widely considered most competent to assert the
claims as to the justice or injustice of actions and arrangements ... [are]
sovereign states."[38] It is this alleged widespread de facto acceptance of
states, above all else, that makes them the "most competent" actors with
respect to justice claims both in and across territorial boundaries. In this
model, governance is not only dominated by sovereign states—they are
the near-exclusive subjects and objects of justice, thus creating, I think,
a liberal vision that is inadequate in today's globalizing world.

One of Carr's more important claims is that international institutions are always subject to being defined according to a contestable status quo by the most powerful and self-serving of actors. As noted above, Carr's worry is that international institutions, and the authoritative practices that structure them, will lose the legitimacy and hence the capacity for promoting peaceful change without a large degree of openness to the justice demands of the less powerful. Certainly Carr was thinking mainly of sovereign states (despite his frequent quasi-Marxist references to class interests); but his critique of any international organization that is closed to justice motives is important also in the context of nonstate actors. In making states the only appropriate subjects and objects of justice, the "statist" model of international governance risks the same problem of being too closed in regard to entitlement claims that are not enshrined in current authoritative practices. This applies not merely to states in international society but also to the justice demands of nonstate actors in addition to the interests of those whose states have failed or are unable to maintain basic rights. This lack of openness to justice claims is a result of an excessive fear of disorder and instability that is exhibited in the work of Welch and, more strongly, of Nardin.

On the surface, Welch is open to incorporating the justice motive of states into increasingly more nuanced, sophisticated, and inclusive authoritative practices and mechanisms. But in the meantime the justice motive is more generally a disruptive feature of world politics. Also in the meantime, Welch contends that any regrettable international situation (we might think of "ethnic cleansing" in Kosovo) or structure (such as the inequalities of globalizing capitalism) that produces a claim to injustice is practically irrelevant when it is unrecognized by authoritative international practice. That is, strictly speaking, the claims of the afflicted can be considered neither just nor unjust: "[W]ithout the appropriate institutional context, there can be no entitlement ... the adjectives 'just' or 'unjust' are misplaced."[39] For this reason, Welch states that cosmopolitan claims for distributive justice or greater global equity are also misplaced and unrealistic. But this reconciles the relationship between moral theory and political practice in a conservative way: That which exists in practice rules out what is most justifiable according to a theory of justice. As Welch contends, the ultimate criterion by which to evaluate a theory of international or global justice is whether it is capable of "enjoying substantial de facto legitimacy across borders."[40] And, "To the extent that there is a legitimate conception of international justice at all, it is embodied and codified in international law."[41] The radical potential of liberalism is thus blunted by embracing the centrality of sovereign states in the process of defining and creating justice.

The underlying conservative and closed nature of this model of international governance is even stronger and more explicit in Nardin. For Nardin, all purposive conceptions of international justice, even among states, are rejected because they necessarily undo and tear asunder the very preconditions of international order. The lesson Nardin reads into the failure of the League of Nations is not, as Carr thought, the need to make international institutions reasonably open to the justice demands of "revisionist" actors. On the contrary, "The arguments about the injustice of the Versailles settlement advanced after World War I mark the beginning toward a conception of international justice as a matter of substantive benefits rather than legality, as having to do above all with the distribution of wealth, power, and other goods among states."[42] The lesson is thus that the introduction of any substantive purposes into international governance is to be resisted in favor of purely formal constraining mechanisms. Questions of redistribution among cosmopolitan lines are thus also rejected—unless they can be handled "indirectly"—as out of hand and beyond the scope of accepted practice.[43]

Classical liberal internationalism's closure to the claims of as yet legally unauthorized entitlements or, more starkly, to purposive conceptions of international right (including issues of redistribution) is highly problematic in today's world. This is particularly so not least because of the challenges to conventional configurations of power, authority, legality, and legitimacy currently wrought by globalization processes. Although Nardin is no doubt correct to insist there is "little evidence" that states will soon disappear,[44] this is no longer the interesting point from the standpoint of justice and today's international institutions. What is interesting is the way in which states, national societies, and markets are being transformed as a consequence of global pressures; what is also interesting is the way in which all actors, state and nonstate, regional, national and transnational, public and private, are framing their actions, reactions, policies, and goals in ways that transcend the purely formal interstate realm that the statist liberal model privileges. The "formal" similarity of external sovereignty cannot, as Nardin hopes, contain the justice motives of a far wider plurality of actors to which I have just alluded.[45]

In the context of globalization, the liberal quest for just authoritative practices should still be a central goal. However, it is misguided and ultimately futile to deny a priori the justice motives of a wide range of actors from affecting the status quo. By remaining open and willing to entertain the informal and the not yet legally recognized justice demands of nonstate actors, liberal theory and institutions could address such phenomena as the protests against the WTO and World Bank mentioned above. This is because, as Richard Devetak and Richard Higgott note, "the voice of the

NGO and GSM [global social movement] is the one serious voice that aspires, rhetorically at least, to the development of a 'justice-based' dialogue beyond the level of the sovereign state."[46] For example, there is little reason not to extend the otherwise excellent analysis that Welch applies to states in war to the recent activities of social movements vis-à-vis multilateral global trading regimes. For example, consider the words of Canadian social activist and global free trade opponent Maude Barlow at the 2001 World Social Forum in Porto Alegre, Brazil: "We should consider this a struggle or war against our governments."[47] This would require, however, that we stop thinking of the so-called justice motive as merely a subjectivist desire by the self (i.e., to receive fair treatment). But such analysis would need to go beyond the statist and formalist bias of liberalism and thereby conceive how and why global social movements make their demands. That is, such movements may demand just treatment for those who cannot voice their own justice demands or those who are structurally excluded from the institutional policy processes of states and international institutions. A liberal statist vision of international governance would have us think that these demands must be ultimately channeled through domestic policy processes anyway.[48] However, as I shall argue in the next chapter, there is reason to think that an exclusively domestic policy approach to these issues is ethically problematic precisely because of the erosion of democratic accountability by globalization processes.

It might be objected that liberal statists have acknowledged that individual human-centric interests have been uneasily integrated into the authoritative practices of international governance through treaties and conventions on human rights. Indeed, Nardin acknowledges that there is profound moral tension between the human rights demands introduced into the legal norms of international society since World War II and the Westphalian framework within which such norms are to be pursued. However, it is important to note his insistence that human dignity is generally better conceived as subordinate to the legal independence of states and thus is to be pursued only "indirectly."[49] The duty of nonintervention and the obligation to observe treaties are among the core, authoritative tenets of international governance as it has evolved in practice.[50] Is there any way, then, to conceive of and respond to the justice demands of ostensibly persecuted collectivities such as the Albanian Kosovars under the Milosovic regime? Under the statist model of global governance, the answer to this would seem to be that the basic rights of these people can be upheld only within the parameters of sovereignty norms claimed by the authorities in Belgrade, and—in the context of the UN Security Council—Moscow and Beijing. If states act outside of these norms, as NATO members did, then their actions cannot be justified by the settled

norms of international society and thus cannot be just.[51] The profound
moral problems with both the conduct and the consequences of NATO's
war over Kosovo cannot be overlooked. The central point here, however,
is that the statist model too easily lends itself to ignoring the justice
motives and claims of nonstate agents, including the persecuted, in favor
of a too complacent stance on the rectitude of the extant rules of international order. If there were and are no easy answers to the moral dilemmas
in Kosovo, the difficult choices faced by state leaders and international
organizations to act more "directly" in favor of basic rights cannot be
merely dismissed as a fundamental misunderstanding of the purely formal nature of international society. Clearly norms are changing and
developing in favor of a "purposive" and active stance, in favor of directly
upholding basic rights. But these norms have to be seriously examined
before being dismissed by liberal statists as simply disruptive and contrary
to the pluralistic essence of international law.

If globalization is a centuries-long process and internationalization, too,
has also long been a feature of the interstate system,[52] it should follow that
global governance, as Craig N. Murphy has aptly shown, is an accurate label
with which to describe the ideological, political, and socioeconomic developments in international organization since the mid-nineteenth century.[53]
But these processes have arguably accelerated recently, thus giving credence
to a variety of poststatist liberal conceptions of international institutionalization. What does shifting from the idea of international governance to
global governance mean? And what should it mean for contemporary
liberal internationalism? It means that international institutions have been
and continue to be affected and transformed by global processes. It also
means that a reconstructed liberal internationalism must allow us to think
beyond the sovereignty of states if it is to be relevant and if it is to achieve
its inner ethico-political goals.

Such a reconstruction is arguably immanent in the recent debates
concerning global governance. Central to these debates are the limitation
of state autonomy and the growing role of nonstate actors. In these
debates there has been more openness to the justice motives of a variety
of actors beyond the state in addition to the concomitant liberal requirement of recognized authoritative practices by which to address conflicting
entitlement claims. As noted, the statist model outlined above is relatively
closed toward entitlement claims that are not currently consolidated into
existing, largely formal authoritative practices. It is also especially closed
to the justice motive as it emerges and operates within the sphere of
nonstate actors. The justice claims of nonstate or societal actors are left to
be sorted out by national governments that are assumed to be legitimate
and capable of determining which principles and procedures are to be

applied in producing a just domestic society.[54] This kind of reasoning informed, for example, many criticisms of the 1998 arrest and detention of former Chilean dictator General Augusto Pinochet by British authorities. International society is no place to pursue the justice motives of individual victims, such critics claimed; only the Chilean polity can come to terms with that.

The dichotomy between the domestic and international spheres found in the statist model is challenged by James N. Rosenau's work on global governance. Rosenau's so-called postinternationalism offers an intriguing analysis of the ethical shortcomings posed by the liberal statist model by proposing to conceive of governance from a new, poststatist "ontology."[55] Rather than "clinging to the notion that states and national governments are the essential underpinnings of the world's organization,"[56] Rosenau claims that the authoritative allocation of values in today's world is affected by a wider plurality of actors and political forces both within and beyond states.[57] Although states are important, international authority has shifted and is changing the role and position of formally sovereign, territorially exclusive units: "[S]tates and governments should be posited not as first among equals, but simply as significant actors in a world marked by an increasing diffusion of authority and a corresponding diminution of hierarchy."[58]

This postinternationalist understanding of global governance opens the door to an ethically reconstructed liberal internationalism, but it is one that Rosenau ultimately fails to enter. Unlike Nardin's, for example, Rosenau's poststatist understanding of world order is not purely formal and closed to the purposive claims of (global) political agents. To the contrary, global governance is defined as the uncontrolled, open-ended, and wide-ranging pursuit of the different purposes, ends, interests, and—one might imagine—entitlement claims by political actors. International organization is thus "more than the formal institutions and organizations through which the management of international affairs is or is not sustained."[59] It is rather a "crazy-quilt" pattern by which agents issue a variety of mutually affecting commands, goals, directives, and policies.[60] "Global governance is [thus] the sum of myriad—literally millions of—control mechanisms driven by different histories, cultures, structures and processes."[61] Actors, sovereign and nonsovereign, are all trying to "satisfy their needs and wants"[62] through the widely available command mechanisms produced by globalization's pressures to integrate and fragment existing states.

Certainly the virtue of this poststatist ontology is that it allows contemporary liberals to entertain the justice motive in a much wider variety of actors and contexts than, say, Welch's statist account. From Rosenau's analysis we could for example view the protests in Seattle against the WTO as an expression of individual and collective subjects' perceptions of a disjuncture between the likely entitlements and material realities produced by a deepened global trading regime. If, as we learn from Carr, an important measure of the legitimacy and effectiveness of international organization is its openness to justice demands, Rosenau's poststatist framework is an improvement. However, merely being attentive to the justice demands of all actors is insufficient for two reasons: First, remaining open to the diverse plurality of all political actors on the globe's surface should not cause us to think that all actors have equal power, legitimacy, and moral authority to make claims or to even voice such claims. As Carr, among others, would remind us: Power differentials permeate politics and existing institutionalization. Rosenau's vision of global governance frequently reads like a reformulated, globalized liberal-pluralism that overlooks if not masks hegemonic practices that exclude the less powerful. Although beyond sovereignty, we are led again to an excessively formal slant on liberal international reform. Hegemonic and top-down practices within globalization prevent the marginalized from legitimately voicing their justice concerns. Rosenau, by contrast, claims that a "disaggregated, decentralized world" is one in which "there is no basis for presuming a pecking order" or any reason to presume that (some) states have a greater or lesser capability to control political outcomes than, say, bond-rating agencies.[63] But global governance is not simply the uncontrolled, open-ended process that Rosenau implies, but something that is patterned by institutions and norms that support certain social forces while excluding others.[64] Moreover, these patterns are still largely structured by state power; as Devetak and Higgott note, "[States] are not mere passive actors in the face of globalization and justice."[65]

Second, and more crucially, the enduring feature of normative international political theory from Carr to Welch and Nardin is that recognizing the justice motive is not enough—there should also be authoritative practices by which to settle entitlement claims. In other words, Rosenau's postinternationalist account of global governance fails to provide a means by which to theorize the development of morally capable institutions—that is, ones amenable to the plethora of justice claims in a poststatist world order. To be clear, it is not that Rosenau fails to envisage future global institutionalization at all.[66] It is, rather, that he fails to consider the moral problems engendered by globalization without the necessary development of global authoritative practices. Without such practices, the international disorder that Welch and Nardin fear, and which Rosenau acknowledges,[67] will become globalized, thus undermining liberal ethico-political values.

There are of course limits and impediments to a poststatist liberal agenda in practice—limits that require sound theoretical and moral principles within a contingent and historically open future world order. These limits are in part exposed by the compelling case for pluralism and cultural diversity that underlies communitarian positions and, by and large, the liberal statist model outlined above.[68] Additionally, these limits are also exposed by the so-called hard cases of contemporary international ethics such as NATO's military intervention in Kosovo. Certainly there is great difficulty in justifying this act by the dominant international authoritative practices of sovereignty and nonintervention; and certainly this particular intervention appeared misconceived, ill-executed, and lacking in impartiality.[69] However, these sad facts do not point to the inherent fallibility of any poststatist model of global governance. To the contrary, I think that they point to the contemporary existence of dynamic processes of norm change currently under way. That is, the NATO action in Kosovo in part *reflects* the inherent problems of (and moral dilemmas created by) acting when international norms are in flux rather than simply contravening an established norm of international law. These emerging norms put claims to sovereignty by state leaders like Milosovic on a highly contingent ground because of a failure to uphold the basic rights of all (in this case, Kosovars) consistently.

Nonetheless, there has yet to develop an appropriate and institutionalized set of authoritative practices to deal with such abuses of human rights outside of the UN system or other regional systems like Europe. Hence, when there is a failure to adapt institutions to emerging norms—as it would seem in this case of the UN—there is an important role for a reconstructed liberal internationalism to guide a reform process. In proposing such theory, we could do no worse than keep Carr's lesson in mind in a globalizing, post-Cold War era: to remain open to justice claims and motives of a wide array of actors in the quest for peaceful change through international organization.

CONCLUSION

In this chapter I have argued that the crisis of liberal internationalism described by Hoffmann cannot be overcome simply by retrenching into a formalistic statism that is too closed to the plethora of justice claims now being made beneath and beyond the current stock of international authoritative practices. I also argued that a reconstructed liberal internationalism would need to pay closer attention to the complexity of achieving justice— as a motive and authoritative practice—in an era of globalization. The crisis of liberal internationalism arises in part because of the tension in today's global order between the justice motives of a variety of state and nonstate actors and the status quo of authoritative practice of international society. In comparing statist models of international governance and poststatist models of global governance, I have argued that the former are too closed to the claims of nonstate actors and to purposive justice claims in general. Nevertheless, while recent poststatist models offer a promising foundation for a reconstructed liberal internationalism, the central tensions between justice as a motive and justice as an authoritative practice will likely persist. As Richard Falk writes, "A feature of international justice in the existing framework of world order is a pervasive need to find balance between contradictory pressures."[70] A reconstructed liberal internationalist practice would aim to balance such pressures with an eye to the principled adaptation and transformation of existing international institutions toward increasingly humane and democratic global practices.

CHAPTER 6

POPULAR SOVEREIGNTY OR COSMOPOLITAN DEMOCRACY? THE FUTURES OF LIBERAL INTERNATIONALISM

> What is desperately needed is a theory that acknowledges the public aspects and effects of ... private activities across borders and establishes a kind of common government for those activities—just as within civil societies liberalism aimed at setting up legitimate institutions in order to rule out the flaws of a "state of nature."
>
> —Stanley Hoffmann[1]

The meaning of liberal internationalism—specifically its vision of progressive reform—is controversial and diverse because of its evolution. Kant's symbolic place within this trajectory is equally complicated by the changing conceptions that liberals have historically held of international politics and the institutionalization of justice. This chapter examines these claims within the context of democratization in the post - Cold War order. There has emerged not merely a revival of liberal internationalist thought, but increasingly refined accounts of the place of democracy in achieving its ethico-political agenda. In particular, there have emerged two scholarly research programs with distinct visions of reform based on the liberal ethical concerns that have been discussed above, freedom and justice. Interestingly, these two visions—the "democratic peace" (DP) thesis and the "cosmopolitan democracy" (CD) model—rely on the contrasting Kantian legacies revealed in chapter 4.

The present chapter compares these liberal visions of reform and makes two central claims. First, like Doyle and Linklater, the DP theorists and CD advocates construct their Kantian foundations from distinct, partial, and often unacknowledged assumptions about the actual nature of Kant's theory of justice. Going beyond this observation, however, I also demonstrate how these distinct understandings of Kant are expressions of the two principal strands of liberal ideology—one classical, the other radical. My second claim is that, in spite of certain weaknesses, the CD model is a superior vision of contemporary reform. Like the statist model of international governance in the last chapter, DP theory is too narrow a basis for such reform because it is constrained by an anachronistic conception of territorially fixed "popular sovereignty." This commitment to popular sovereignty actually arises from an uncritical acceptance of Kant's seemingly rigorous formalism in his theory of justice. This formal vision of the conditions of reform constrains the potential for autonomy in a context of globalization. The CD model, by contrast, draws upon other elements from Kant in an attempt to transcend the limiting role that sovereignty plays in his political thought. In place of popular sovereignty, it is Kant's (admittedly vague) notion of "cosmopolitan law" that CD theorists employ to depict the type of reforms required to promote autonomy under globalizing conditions. Although this model exaggerates the role of cosmopolitan law in Kant's thought, the attempt is nonetheless a genuine reflection of his vision that material factors, too, are required to achieve justice.

The reason it is possible to use Kantian precepts to support two very distinct visions of reform derives from the ambiguity inherent in his theory of justice discussed in previous chapters. This ambiguity goes to the heart of why his legacy has become ammunition for both classical and radical internationalists. As argued above, Kant makes a categorical distinction between politics and morality by explicitly stating that justice concerns only formal principles of Right and not material principles of virtue.[2] From this, his claim that states must create and maintain consistent domains of external freedom for individuals by refraining from imposing ends to which they would not consent is justified. When classical liberals interpret Kant, however, they take this rigidly stated formalism to vindicate such ideas as "limited government" and mere "equality of right." In the analysis below I claim that the DP theorists absorb this classical liberal stance vis-à-vis Kant's meaning because they simply apply it, by analogy, to the relations among states. That is, they seek only to ensure that states act like individuals in liberal domestic society by recognizing formal principles of noninterference; and the way in which this is accomplished is through the mechanism of democracy inside the state, operating in much the same formal manner.

But the classical liberal reading of Kant's theory of justice is, I shall claim, partial and potentially misleading. This is because Kant's intention is merely to prevent attempts by the state or certain sectors of society from imposing their conceptions of "virtue" upon autonomous individuals (for whom moral action requires a purely "inner" inspiration).[3] As claimed above, there are indications that Kant conceived justice as having not only a formal basis, but also a material one. That is, reform is not merely about approximating the purely transcendental principles of Right—it is also about activating and promoting certain material purposes or ends in the political world that correspond to and enable autonomy.[4]

Radical liberals have thus followed the less well defined elements of Kant's theory of justice that suggest that once the basic, formal principles of external liberty have been realized, individual "welfare" is important too. This type of reading of Kant is what tacitly sustains the CD theorists' use of his legacy; for they hold that we ought not merely assume that a Rightful condition among states is the purpose of international reform. They also hold that the formal sovereignty of states must not subordinate the direct realization of individual autonomy because globalization means that its realization is affected by material factors that are not, ultimately, territorially fixed.

In both research programs the concept of "democracy" is central. In DP theory it is the regime type that causes peace among similarly constituted states. In the CD model, however, democracy is not merely a type of constitution—it is a principle of governance that actualizes autonomy in a diversity of settings, local, national, and transnational. But this democratic preoccupation is ultimately a strange thing to combine with Kant's philosophy because, as noted previously, he explicitly condemns democracy as "necessarily a despotism," a form of rule that is entirely incompatible with freedom and perpetual peace.[5] On the one hand, this suggests a large measure of superficiality on the part of contemporary liberals who fail to differentiate between "the ideas of republicanism, liberalism and populism in his writings."[6] On the other hand, a much more interesting possibility—one that I consider in this chapter—is that the peculiar connotations of democracy within DP and CD scholarship are being used for ideological purposes: either to support or deny the central role that state sovereignty has traditionally played within liberal internationalist reform projects.

THE DEMOCRATIC PEACE THESIS: POPULAR SOVEREIGNTY
AND INTERNATIONAL REFORM

The popularity of the DP thesis can be measured by the vast literature it has inspired. Indeed, with the remarkable degree of consensus on the theoretical significance of the "law" that democracies do not fight each other, some speak of the DP as if it has achieved the status of "normal science" in International Relations.[7] In this section I describe the context from which the DP thesis became popularized and explain the limited way it draws upon Kant's legacy. For he is invoked to account for and justify an extremely narrow conception of international reform. My analysis is restricted to the assumptions and claims of the most influential contributors to the DP scholarship. Although there are some differences among them, there is an implicitly shared commitment to "popular sovereignty" as a sufficient mechanism of international reform.

Although there were a few scholars working on the connection between democratic forms of government and interstate peace in the 1970s, it was, as noted above, Doyle's work of the early 1980s that first created the impression that Kant anticipated and explained the current reality of liberal interstate peace.[8] However, it was not until after the Cold War that such a scholarly practice became so widely diffused. The practical significance of the so-called Kantian vision that democratic regimes objectively enjoy pacific relations became salient once the Soviet Union collapsed and a wave of democratization swept the world.

In the most prominent DP literature of the early 1990s there are several references to Wilson's legacy. He, too, is said to have anticipated the idea of democratic pacification in a manner similar to that of Kant. Indeed, as Russett claims, Wilson's Fourteen Points read as though they could have been penned by Kant.[9] Given the profound scorn heaped upon Wilsonianism during the realist-dominated Cold War years, his rehabilitation required a few adjustments by contemporary DP scholars. Charles W. Kegley Jr., for example, claims that Wilson's ideas were not flawed; he was just too ahead of his time for them to have any impact.[10] Similarly, Russett claims that Wilson's ideals, as those of Kant's, could not be adequately tested, much less made to function, in a world in which too few democracies existed.[11] However, a "new world order" has produced an opportune context. As Chan describes it, "In the wake of the 'third wave' of democratizing, democracies constitute for the first time a majority of the states in the international system."[12] This fact has provided the impetus for the neo-Wilsonian spirit that has penetrated not only the speeches of American presidents in the 1990s, but the International Relations academy.[13] However, whereas Wilson's credo was that of "making the world safe for democracy," the proponents of the DP thesis suggest only "making the world safe through democracy." In other words, democracy is viewed as an independent variable creating peace, rather than an institution that grounds individual freedom and justice.

This fundamental constriction of the Wilsonian world-view is largely conceded by some DP theorists. For example, Russett claims that the current world order favors an attempt on the part of liberal-minded advocates of peace to make exclusive use of democratization as a technique of pacification. He adds that the old "idealist" program from the early twentieth century was rightly tossed aside. The mechanisms of collective security "as embodied in the League of Nations," international law, and any other such ideals associated with Wilson are tested but failed relics. "But the elements of [free] trade and democracy," however, "were never given a fair chance."[14] The relative absence of economic nationalism and the formal commitment to democracy by the majority of states today are viewed as the supreme terms of liberal internationalist reform for the present era. Theoretically, however, what is occurring here is a radical truncation of the Wilsonian legacy. But this very same pattern is evident in the way DP theorists draw on Kant, as will be demonstrated below. Nonetheless, the one aspect of Kant's and Wilson's intellectual legacies that is actually maintained is the notion of "popular sovereignty" as the path to peace (rather than democracy per se).

Ruminations on intellectual foundations occupy only a small place in the DP literature. As a more or less coherent research program, its advocates are more interested in the rigorous construction and testing of theory. The widely accepted fact that "democracies" have not engaged in "war," as variously defined by DP theorists, requires an explanation. Once this explanation is established as valid through testing, it garners profound significance for assessing the nature of international politics. As Doyle and Russett claim, if democracy indeed causes peace, it would discredit the realist claim that the anarchic structure of the state system determines the nature of relations among units.[15] In other words, if the DP theorists' main hypothesis is verified, the democratic constitution of states can overcome the anarchy in which they are allegedly situated.

The most controversy sparked by the DP thesis has been whether its advocates have really proved that it is democracy, and not some other variable, that is responsible for existent pacific interstate relations. Several critics have claimed that the DP thesis actually has "extremely little explanatory power,"[16] and some have provided a host of alternative explanations for the appearance of peace among liberal democratic states.[17] As Chan writes, such critics normally argue that the statistical results confirming the DP thesis depend upon dubious "definitions of democracy and war." Moreover, the majority of critics "suggest that the generalizability of the phenomenon is limited to specific spatial and temporal domains (the North Atlantic Area or the Cold War era)."[18] In response, DP theorists such as Russett and John Owen have maintained that peace among democracies is caused by features intrinsic to democracy or liberalism, "rather than being caused exclusively by economic or geopolitical characteristics correlated with democracy."[19]

Although I share the skepticism that many have expressed about the DP thesis, the dominant issues of its theoretical exactitude and empirical validity are of secondary importance in this chapter.[20] Of more crucial significance is how this research program as a whole, and the way it has been carefully circumscribed by its main proponents, shapes and constrains the contemporary debate about the limits of liberal internationalist reform. Equally important is the way in which the limited vision of such reformist measures—including both the nature of the means used and the ends sought—is used to selectively constitute a Kantian legacy that is then represented as a prior foundation for reform. The ease with which DP theorists (and many of their critics) have crammed Kant's political philosophy into a simplistic causal relationship between democracy and peace is remarkable. There is often little or no appreciation of the markedly different historical context in which Kant's texts were written, and even less consideration of the larger philosophical edifice that grounds his perpetual peace project. Most DP theorists write as though Kant shared exactly the same political and analytical concerns as they, and as if his texts were therefore written with the same intentions that contemporary self-described liberals hold.[21] One group of critics has stated this problem forcefully:

> It is a sad testimony to the state of DP theorizing that so many authors hurriedly genuflect in front of the rumored content of his essay ["Perpetual Peace"] before delving into their inductive pursuits. Kant's essay is the tip of a complex Enlightenment iceberg. It should be read more carefully before it is extolled as a trivial idol.[22]

Nonetheless, it is important to consider just what elements of Kant's thought are actually being selectively absorbed. Although DP theorists attempt to draw upon a rather partial Kantian legacy, they absorb and endorse certain elements of his theory of justice that render their prescriptions for international reform extraordinarily limited.

The DP vision of Kant seems to be shaped by the post-Cold War context in which a very specific type of liberal international reform has become available. For example, on the one hand Russett speaks of the triumph of the "values of economic and especially political freedom" as something validating Kant's vision, making him the most relevant available philosophical foundation.[23] Russett thinks that

> [w]hen democratic states were rare, the Kantian perspective had little practical import, and power politics reigned. But if the Kantian perspective is correct, recent events replacing authoritarian regimes with democratic values and institutions in much of Asia, Eastern Europe, and Latin America may have profound significance not just for governmental practices, but for worldwide peace among states.[24]

And yet, as this statement suggests, Kant's meaning is being radically shorn and stripped down to fit the contemporary expectations that Russett and other DP theorists hold. Leaving aside for a moment the fact that Kant thought his perspective had validity *in spite* of the existence of numerous democratic regimes, it is crucial to recall that his vision of international reform does not rely merely upon one single, domestically based mechanism. DP theorists are thus engaged in reducing Kant's reform project to the single mechanism of popular government within the sovereign state. With the notable exception of Doyle—for whom Kant's philosophy of history is also of crucial importance—the tendency has been to assume that Kant believed democracy to be a sufficient cause of peaceful and just interstate relations.[25] As noted above, Russett suggests that all "idealist" notions of international law, federalism, or interstate peace leagues are discredited by the experiences of the twentieth century. This is likely why he and other DP theorists practically ignore the second and third definitive articles of Kant's hypothetical peace treaty, that is, they overlook his confederation of states and the ideal of cosmopolitan law. Indeed, if and when the practical content of these articles is implied, it is quickly subordinated to the first definitive article, assumed to be coextensive with democracy: "Other influences, such as trade and a network of international law and organizations, as suggested by Kant, likely also play a role in directly *supplementing* and *strengthening* that of democracy."[26] Many critics have pointed out that Kant's project does not rely on such a slim basis as the spread of formally democratic state structures around the globe to produce peace.[27] As Gates and colleagues state, "the key to perpetual peace does not lie with one single factor, but in a complex web of things."[28] But the Kantian legacy that DP theorists have consciously selected, that is, the democratic constitution, cannot be taken in abstraction from other elements of his thought.

To be clear, the point here is not simply that DP theorists should also consider the importance of the other mechanisms in Kant's texts.

The concern, rather, is with the ideological and theoretical effects of taking a "part" of his legacy and representing it as the "whole" nature of contemporary liberal international reform. By embracing almost exclusively the first definitive article of "Perpetual Peace," the tradition is being radically abbreviated in favor of a type of classical liberalism. The tendency of DP scholars to reiterate the reformative powers of democracy is misleading if one examines closely the underlying assumptions they make about how it functions. It transpires that, rather than democracy per se, what is being advocated as a palliative for international anarchy is simply a form of popular sovereignty (albeit one that ideally includes a set of constitutional divisions that are advocated by philosophers such as Kant). Doyle, for example, states that in order

> [t]o ensure that morally autonomous individuals remain free in those areas of social action where public authority is needed, public legislation has to express the *will of the people making laws for their own communities* ... the effective sovereigns of the state are [therefore] representative legislators deriving their authority from the consent of the *electorate and exercising* their authority *free from all restraint* apart from the requirement that basic civil rights be preserved.[29]

Democracy appears to be the more palatable contemporary shorthand for a peculiarly liberal configuration of internal sovereignty. As Doyle adds, under popular rule, "the state is subject to neither the external authority of other states nor the internal authority of special prerogatives held, for example, by monarchs or military castes over policy."[30] The DP theorists thus express the classical liberal internationalist hope that the external sovereignty of states will be exercised with more restraint—and anarchy will thereby be mitigated—when internal sovereignty is located in the people.

There are two kinds of problems that emerge from the attempt by DP theorists to restrict the terms of international reform to simply that of a system of sovereign states checked by the desires of their *demoi*. One set of problems can be imagined simply by reinserting this mechanism within the context of the Kantian philosophical edifice from which it was abstracted. On the one hand, it is grossly naive to assume that the so-called people are pacific. Kant himself seems to set the standard for naiveté in his notorious statement, noted in chapter 3, to the effect that citizens are inherently pacific under the right constitution.[31] On the other hand, his comment is so often taken out of context because Kant is not speaking about democracy but "republicanism," as a specific "form of sovereignty"[32] that he assumes democracy to be incapable of achieving. This republican "form" divides state power between executive and legislative branches whilst a united *demos* cannot, he asserts, be so divided. There is hence a problem with assuming that Kantian precepts support the DP hypothesis—he did not believe that merely placing the controls over foreign policy in the hands of the people will pacify state conduct. Additionally, Kant does not claim to reveal a general law about republics but simply a propensity for such states to be more pacific; he did not claim that republics would necessarily abstain from fighting each other.

Even if—as it is sometimes argued by DP scholars—democracy is nowadays more or less the same as Kant's understanding of republicanism, a second problem arises. "Perpetual Peace" does not rest only on the first definitive article or republican sovereignty for a good reason: In his mind all forms of sovereignty, whether republican or democratic, are situated in a context of anarchy in which states have little incentive or opportunity to reform. As claimed above, Kant does not think that states are likely to merely will reform. By exaggerating the reformative potential of popularly controlled, and of course constitutionally divided, government in Kant's thought, DP theorists ignore all of those aspects in his texts that are skeptical of the capacity of *any* form of the sovereign state to reform.

It is unsurprising that Kant makes the *form* of governments and of states the chief concern of the first definitive article. It reflects his philosophical bias to the effect that formal principles are always logically prior to material ones when framing political reform. As noted in chapter 3, Kant claims that the problem of injustice is initially solved by the mere existence of a sovereign capable of overcoming the state of nature domestically; it is the only a priori condition that is absolutely required before any material conditions of justice can be sought. This is because, formally at least, a sovereign is the only agent that can provide for equal domains of external liberty in society; but if Kant's theory of justice is limited—as it is by some scholars[33]—to this purely formal dimension, a rather complacent liberalism necessarily results. A minimalist state would effectively reach the *telos* of individual freedom and terminate reform. Classical liberals in political theory typically argue that domestic political reform stops at the ethical limits of Kant's formalism; and as a consequence, they fail to envisage ways in which actually existing liberal states fail to achieve anything more than mere negative liberty.

The DP literature is similar in its complacency about what forms of governance are adequate to human freedom in today's globalizing world. By overlooking the second and third definitive articles, in which Kant gives some reasons for going beyond the framework of the purely formal principles of republican sovereignty, DP theorists reproduce the assumptions of classical liberals. Because they so closely identify democracy with popular sovereignty, the DP scholars limit contemporary liberal internationalist reform to the extant framework of territorial states. Democracy in this sense only reinforces the statist framework of international relations, a grid that we know Kant realized cannot ultimately satisfy the conditions of individual freedom—the actually existing sovereign state, in addition to the state system, is never completely reformed such that individual autonomy can be said to have been fully achieved. But, as argued in earlier chapters, a more complete understanding of Kant's theory of justice reveals that he goes beyond his initial formalism to consider how the material requirements of autonomy must also be satisfied. DP theorists appear to take the view that the most minimal conditions of democratic control over foreign policy are the effective *telos* of international reform. For example, Doyle writes that the Kantian view of "political society" is one that has already, "from a formal-legal point of view, solved the problem of combining moral autonomy, individualism, and social order."[34] Russett, too, conceives the formal structures of actually existing, democratic procedures and safeguards as sufficient to international reform.[35] Moreover, as Chan notes, "researchers analyzing the democratic peace have shown a greater interest in the spatial spread of formally democratic structures than in their temporal resilience."[36]

To summarize the points above, rather than simply taking the ideal of democracy from Kant's legacy, DP theorists have really taken (out of context) that element of his thinking dedicated to popular sovereignty. But what they are actually absorbing from the first definitive article is his view that a popular form of sovereignty is a cause of peace. Thus the DP theorists take from Kant's legacy only his initially strict formalism that is a part of his theory of justice. As claimed above, however, there is potential tension between such formal principles of justice and material principles in Kant's thought. For while he consistently places a priority upon formal causes, he also places great stock in a principle of enlightenment. This principle is the historically dynamic ideal that material causes and purposes have a progressively greater role in determining the political structures that are initially only formal.[37]

The DP theorists' attempt to take Kant's vision of the popular sovereignty mechanism from "Perpetual Peace" does not merely do injustice to his larger political philosophy, it is an inadequate basis for contemporary reform. By following the classical liberal tendency to restrict justice to the purely formal dimensions of his legacy, international transformation is limited to that of regulating relations among democratic states (or, more ambitiously, to that of expanding the circle of democracies). Indeed, such states are treated in DP theory as largely analogous to individuals in classical liberalism—without, of course, the overarching sovereign. As a result, where formal democracy prevails, the same complacency noted above vis-à-vis the requirements of domestic reform is reproduced at the international level. As Doyle claims, "International peace is not a utopian idea to be reached, if at all, in the far future; it is a condition that liberal states have already experienced in their relations with each other."[38] Moreover, if liberal internationalist reform is restricted to the purely formal realm of interstate peace among constitutional democracies, there is the implication that individual freedom or autonomy is satisfied within the institutional machinery of each sovereign state. However, by looking merely at the formal external relations of sovereign democratic states, the DP theorists are blind to a massive range of material changes in the world that must be addressed before any celebrations of having completed liberal internationalism's agenda can begin.

COSMOPOLITAN DEMOCRACY AND LIBERAL INTERNATIONALIST REFORM

In this section I claim that the CD model, as developed by a handful of theorists, is a substantial and novel contribution to liberal internationalism, one that is ultimately superior to the DP approach. In the main, advocates of this approach do not employ the terms "liberalism" or "internationalism" to describe their position. This does not impose a tremendous barrier to my argument, however. On the one hand, it is perhaps because liberalism is so widely associated with a sovereign state-based program for reform that CD scholars have had little incentive to use such labels. On the other, however, the inspiration of the CD project is compatible with the ethical aims of liberalism in general, albeit a liberalism that is reformulated to reflect better the requirements of individual autonomy in a changed political context. Indeed, the model is more compatible with a tradition of radical or reform liberalism because, in this strand of ideology, democracy has never been coeval with popular sovereignty but is associated with expanding citizenship to include once-marginalized sectors of society and with promoting equality of opportunity and outcome. Indeed, the chief exponent of the CD model, David Held, has characterized himself as a liberal-socialist.[39]

In many ways, CD theory continues the tradition of nonstatist forms of international liberalism discussed in the previous chapter. The liberal internationalism implied by the CD research program is one that is skeptical of the assumption that the liberal democratic state can be the exclusive anchor of individual autonomy in the present world. In place of territorially based popular sovereignty, CD theorists speculate on the possibility of several overlapping, nonterritorial forms of democratic

governance that would both restrict and complement the existence of formally sovereign states. Held's book, *Democracy and the Global Order*,[40] is
perhaps the most complete elaboration to date on this approach; but
other scholars such as Daniele Archibugi and Linklater have added important insights to its meaning.[41]

All three of these authors connect Kant's legacy to the possibility of
nonstatist frameworks of international reform that are designed to promote freedom in a radically changing, globalizing context. As with the DP
theorists, CD proponents appear to frame their understanding of Kant's
legacy in the light of how they view the post-Cold War world. Held, for
example, shares the sense of optimism found within DP scholarship about
the dramatic increase in democratic regimes in the recent past. However,
he is much less sanguine about the extent to which this phenomenon ful-
fills the liberal aim of freedom or autonomy. Quite simply, CD theorists
argue that the increase in the number of formally democratic states worldwide is of limited significance in a globalizing world order.[42] Indeed, what
distinguishes them from mainstream liberal internationalists is that they
do not look merely at the formal structures of governments, but also at the
material changes introduced into the world by transnational processes
that go beyond the limited reach of any particular sovereign state.

Archibugi and Held enumerate several important phenomena in the
post-Cold War era that have been ignored by DP theorists, phenomena that
point to the crisis of liberal internationalism discussed in the last chapter.
First, "despite the geographic extension of liberal democratic regimes, ...
for millions of people there has been no noticeable improvement—and
in some cases drastic reduction—in the quality of their political associations."[43] Second, disintegrative forces within the state—the Yugoslav case
being the most salient example—have been unleashed and intensified
throughout the past decade. As Held notes, "local groups, movements and
nationalisms are questioning the nation-state from below as the representative and accountable power system."[44] Indeed, it is the failure of liberal
democracy to include a diversity of women, indigenous peoples, and the
poor that has in some cases led to such challenges. Thus the ability of states
to effectively maintain "domestic peace and the protection of the safety of
their citizens and those citizens' property" is increasingly questioned by
disaffected groups that, at the very least, want increased autonomy and
recognition of their cultural specificity.[45] Perhaps most crucially, despite
the recent increase in the number of democratic regimes, the existing institutional structure of interstate affairs has been remarkably recalcitrant to
reform. That is, the major democracies have been unwilling "to extend
their model of governance to interstate relations ... [and are reluctant] to
be called into account on matters of security and foreign affairs."[46]

As these points suggest, the CD theorists do not see the emerging reality of post-Cold War international politics to be worthy of the complacent stance the DP advocates appear to have taken regarding reform. This is principally because they do not look merely at the formal structure of state constitutions as the most significant basis for judging the current nature of international politics. As a result, a more complicated, and not necessarily optimistic, picture comes into focus. The notion of popular sovereignty loses its appeal and cannot be conflated, as the DP theorists appear to do, with a commitment to full, inclusive democracy. This is to say that it is not merely that it is naive to think that popular sovereignty is a sufficient mechanism for peace, as realists have complained. It is, rather, that the classical liberal assumptions about this concept have not, in fact, included in the definition of the "popular" several marginalized groups from within or, it transpires, from across states. Additionally, the acceleration of processes of globalization render existing, territorially rooted notions of popular sovereignty inadequate because of the resultant decrease in the autonomy of states. Even popularly elected governments cannot respond to the interests of those to whom they are accountable because they are enmeshed in processes that they lack the power or incentive to halt. Thus, independent states can no longer be the sole instrument of promoting individual freedom. The formalism of the DP research program leads it to consider only the legal reality of each state's independent constitution, that is, its sovereignty.[47] Consequently, the erosion of the state's actual autonomy because of globalization is ignored.[48] By contrast, the CD theorists hold that the increased transborder flows of goods, money, advertising images, and cultural commodities attest to the increased power of multinational corporations and financial markets. Additionally, there is increased attention to the environmental, health, and migrant-population crises. These things are largely the effects of the interconnections between states and societies that are being rapidly intensified and "mediated by such phenomena as modern communication networks and new information technology."[49]

If democratic control of the institutions of governance creates the conditions of individual freedom, globalization poses a profound crisis even for classical liberal democratic precepts.[50] The assumed conjunction of democracy and territoriality that animates the ideal of popular sovereignty is under increased assault in our daily, concrete experience. As Held claims,

> Some of the most fundamental forces and processes that determine the nature of life chances within and across political communities are now beyond the reach of individual nation-states. The system of national

political communities persists of course, but it is articulated and rearticulated today with complex economic, organizational, administrative, legal,
and cultural processes and structures that limit and check its efficacy. If
these processes are not acknowledged and brought into political processes
themselves, they may bypass or circumvent the democratic state system.[51]

There are several gaps between traditional liberal internationalist expectations, such as those found in DP theory, and actual material circumstances—each of which points to a net decrease in the choice that
individuals exercise over the ends and obligations that are imposed
upon them. Formal state authorities have decreasing control over actual
economic systems; sovereign states can little evade the incentives to par-
ticipate in the management of problems through intergovernmental
organizations and regimes;[52] citizenship in national communities, and
the rights and duties upon which it is constituted, fails to match "the
development of regional and international law which subject individuals,
nongovernmental organizations and governments to new systems of reg-
ulation."[53] From these observations CD theorists make a fundamentally
Kantian claim: that the realization of freedom within a domestic context
is always contingent upon and made vulnerable by international (and now
global) forces.[54]

Therefore, it is not merely the prospect of interstate violence that is the
threat to freedom—it is a much more complex and widespread set of ends
that are being imposed upon individuals without their consent or participation that is the main concern of CD advocates.[55] The neo-Wilsonian
notion of making the world safe for democracy is replaced with the more
radical ideal of democratizing world politics by supplementing the already
emerging system of global governance with representative mechanisms.
What is advocated is the reconceptualization and fortification of democracy
"both within preestablished borders and across them."[56] The "constitutive
principles of democracy such as respect for minorities, the independence
of judicial power and the guarantee of fundamental rights" should be internationalized to overcome the gaps identified above.[57] What the CD model
represents, then, is a much more ambitious and expanded vision of liberal
internationalist reform. Its proposals involve the development of global
channels of democratic representation and legitimacy and the eventual
restriction of sovereign state power. This model is unlike previous federal-
ist models in that it seeks neither to "abolish existing states nor replace
their powers with an entirely different institutional framework."[58] Such an
attempt would be futile anyway in light of the nationalist pressures and
cultural particularities that challenge existing states. Rather, existing states
would be " 'relocated' within an overarching democratic law."[59] As I argue

below, the CD model goes far beyond what Kant would advocate, despite the fact that his ideal of "cosmopolitan law" is its inspiration. This is because sovereign states would eventually be legally subordinate to cosmopolitan democratic law:

> What is necessary is to deprive states of some of their more coercive and restrictive powers: in the former case, those powers that are deployed against the welfare and safety of citizens; in the latter case, those powers which are deployed to forestall or inhibit collaborative relations among states on pressing international questions.[60]

Obviously this type of change in the nature of international politics would be profound. We need only think of the recent reluctance of the United States, the self-perceived leader of the democratic free world, to agree to the provisions of the new permanent International Criminal Court or the Ottawa Treaty to ban antipersonnel land mines to realize this.[61]

Many elements of the CD model are not entirely innovative. As noted above, the model is to an extent an updated and global version of radical liberalism in comparison with the classical liberal internationalism of the DP theorists. Although the CD theorists advocate restrictions to sovereignty that exceed what many other liberals are willing to countenance, they are also actually interested in bringing under control or domesticating certain elements of global civil society that wield massive amounts of unaccountable power, such as multinational corporations. Thus the restrictions to state sovereignty envisaged by the CD model do not jettison the idea of popular control over governmental institutions altogether. On the contrary, claims Held, "*Sovereignty is an attribute of the basic democratic law, but it could be entrenched and drawn upon in diverse self-regulating associations, from states to cities and corporations*," all without the illusion that each of these agents can remain entirely autonomous from a cosmopolitan legal order.[62]

Such statements resemble the nonstatist orientation of Mitrany, who, as noted in chapter 4, can be read as advocating a reformed liberal internationalism that anticipates the concerns, if not the actual proposals, of Held and his collaborators.[63] Interestingly, the CD theorists do not claim this more recent and perhaps more obvious connection to reform liberals in the international realm. They instead go back much further for theoretical antecedents: "For more than three centuries, thinkers ... have sought to create international institutions capable of acting as arbiters between states and, in the final analysis, as the foundation of a legally based international relations."[64] The "thinkers" in question include Émeric Cruré, Abbé de Saint-Pierre, Rousseau, and Bentham among others. However, it is the legacy of Kant that CD theorists have invoked most frequently. As is the case with the DP thesis, the presentation of Kant's meaning and significance is affected by the way in which this particular group of scholars views the present world order. Kant's legacy is thus situated within a concern CD theorists have with building institutions transnationally that will enhance individual autonomy.

Nonetheless, it should be noted that the CD theorists recognize that Kant's texts also pose some serious limitations as a guide for new visions of contemporary reform. As Linklater, for example, points out, "Imagining ways in which individuals could come together as world citizens who participated in joint rule was not one of Kant's concerns and it has hardly been central to the subsequent political theory of the interliberal peace."[65] CD scholars thus consciously aim to transcend Kant while preserving those features of his thought that can be adapted for present purposes; what is interesting is the way in which they seek to do this.

The CD theorists go beyond Kant's actual international reform project as it is articulated in "Perpetual Peace." Although they do not describe their rejection of certain elements of Kantian justice in the following terms, it is clearly the effect of their redescription of his legacy. For the transnational institutional frameworks of democratic law that they propose actually violate the a priori terms of Kant's theory of justice. It must be recalled that the confederation of states that Kant proposes is a loose, voluntary association that serves little purpose other than the avoidance of war.[66] There is no independent, representative body over and above the contingent wills of the sovereigns. Although the CD model does not wish to eliminate states, it clearly removes the discretion they have to make exceptions for themselves from international agreements and rules that Kant ultimately leaves them. As Held notes, although the democratic transnational institutions that the CD model envisages would initially require the popular consent of national communities, thereafter the agreements reached would be legally binding.[67] The representatives of these overlapping institutions would serve their constituents rather than merely their national governments.

But what about the danger of "soulless despotism" that Kant believed would accompany any attempt at supranational state building or world government?[68] The CD theorists acknowledge this by noting that Kant did not see how anything wider than a state could be a feasible system of representative rule.[69] But this argument is potentially misleading. Kant's objection to supranational institutions is much deeper than a concern with feasibility. As we know, he simply held as dogma the view that an effective and functioning system of justice could rely upon only one illimitable legislator, the sovereign. He could not envisage the overlapping, mutually constitutive relations among different governmental bodies encompassing many states, even though his republicanism should have logically demanded something similar within the state. Nonetheless, Held thinks that any "Kantian" objections about the potential despotism of supranational democratic institutions of governance can be overcome: "[Cosmopolitan democracy] connotes nothing more or less than the entrenchment of and enforcement of democratic public law across all peoples—a binding framework for the political business of states and societies and regions, *not a detailed regulative framework for the direction of all their affairs.*"[70]

The priority of formal principles over material causes in Kant's theory of justice would seem to be the greatest impediment to making his thought commensurable with the CD model, or any other nonstatist schemes of global reform for that matter. As Laberge claims, many neo-Kantian scholars have attempted to redefine his thought with an eye to issues of global distributive justice and the plight of the suffering, that is, human needs.[71] However, Laberge asserts that they overlook Kant's view that all political relations must be justified and organized around principles that scrupulously ignore such material realities. That is, Kant's initial view of justice requires only the observance of the legal conditions of external liberty, even if certain undesired material ends are permitted to exist or are created.[72] From this more "conservative" (i.e., literal) interpretation of Kant's philosophical meaning, we are required to discount the novel material constellations that are being produced by globalization. The progressive increase in the flows of communication and commerce across state boundaries and the realization of novel intergovernmental and supranational political and legal institutions are all irrelevant from a strictly formal reading of Kantian justice. The DP scholars follow this narrower realization of Kant's legacy.

However, Laberge's insistence on taking Kant's formalism seriously should not be taken too far. That is, we can recognize the priority of formalism within Kant's thought and still imagine—as did he—the ways in which the material factors of politics gain an increasingly greater significance to the organization and justification of political institutions. Indeed, this is the reading of Pogge. In his view, Kant's understanding of enlightenment should be viewed as a process in which the material ends of politics progressively gain greater consideration. This process is enhanced through time as the solidification of legitimate mechanisms of conflict resolution among individuals and states becomes increasingly accepted and habitually respected.[73] As the anarchy problématique fades—both domestically and internationally—the material ends constitutive of individual autonomy become increasingly important to the realization of justice. Viewed from this perspective, the CD model may actually realize a crucial dimension of Kant's legacy just as it tacitly transcends its formalism and the dogmatic statism it sustains. To be sure, the line between interpretation and revisionism of Kant's thought is fuzzy, but there is much incentive to err on the side of making his legacy relevant. A fundamental insight of Kant's political theory is that individual freedom is not only determined by the conditions of domestic politics, but by causes outside of the state. This insight is not altered by globalization; it is, rather, made more complicated because the constructed distinction between the "inside" and the "outside" of states—a barrier that Kant's thought contributes to as much as it tries to overcome it—is increasingly untenable.[74]

The CD theorists have thus understandably emphasized what is perhaps the most innovative and least understood elements in Kant's international reform project: the idea of cosmopolitan law that is outlined in the third definitive article of "Perpetual Peace."[75] Whereas the DP theorists almost entirely construe Kant's relevance through the lens of the first definitive article, the CD advocates have nearly done the same with the third. What Kant actually claims in this article is that states must grant hospitable treatment to foreign individuals on their soil because people hold certain inalienable rights; and he condemns colonialism and slavery. Kant states that this cosmopolitan law is not a "utopian" or unrealistic thing, but a distinct supplement to state and international law.[76] According to CD theorists, this rather sketchy set of statements "decidedly broadens the theoretical statements on juridical pacifism," and in a way that overcomes the traditionally statist and undemocratic nature of interstate relations hitherto advocated by liberals.[77]

On the one hand it is tempting to include the CD theorists with others that Onuf states "have made much of Kant's cosmopolitanism—perhaps too much."[78] On the other, however, CD theorists readily concede that Kant's cosmopolitan law at best anticipates what they advocate because, in the end, "he failed to indicate the means whereby cosmopolitan law was to be enforced."[79] The reconstruction of Kant's notion of cosmopolitan law may well serve as a practical ideal in proposing alternative forms of democratic governance and international reform. However, this particular explanation about why it appears in so limited and rudimentary a form in Kant's actual texts is also unconvincing because it is not grounded in a full appreciation of his theory of justice. Although it is certainly true that Kant provides the grounds for thinking about cosmopolitan citizenship as the embodiment of the moral kingdom of ends, the "dogma" of sovereignty is, in my view, the actual cause of his unwillingness to articulate a means of its enforcement. Ultimately, Kant's international reform project relies upon state action and discretion, and thus cosmopolitanism is a *moral* rather than *political* phenomenon.[80] Thus, it is not merely that Kant failed to complete his picture of an enforceable cosmopolitan law: it is rather that, had he done so, he would have certainly contradicted the content of his other definitive articles. What is missing is a more explicit account of why a critical reconstruction of Kant's limited and ultimately statist international reform project is necessary. Such a critique is necessary if his vision of cosmopolitan law is to be reconstructed in a way that is adequate for contemporary global politics.

CONCLUSION

This chapter has compared two distinct research programs that advocate reform in global politics. I have suggested that these programs are animated by contrasting types of liberal ideology that draw upon Kantian foundations. One potential problem with this exercise is stated by Onuf: "That Kant came to conclusions that liberals now identify with does not mean that he started from liberal premises. ... Any such reading of Kant is highly anachronistic."[81] It is certainly true that Kant would not have recognized the concept of "liberalism." Nonetheless, his international reform project anticipates the concerns of a subsequent tradition of liberals, and, more crucially, his legacy has been consistently employed as an ideological tool to redefine the nature of this tradition.

After the Cold War, the dominant liberal internationalist vision of reform in International Relations has been the DP thesis. Although DP scholars have maintained a limited focus on the causal relationship between democracy and peace, their use of Kant as a foundation reveals that there is also an ideological core of classical liberalism behind their scientific pursuits. A bias arises from restricting liberal reform to the mechanism of popular sovereignty, which is only one of the paths to peace advocated by Kant. This limited focus is a result of a tendency of DP theorists to absorb only the formal principles of his political theory. As a consequence, the reform prescribed by this approach is too limited and state-centric to satisfy autonomy in an era of globalization.

As I have demonstrated, the CD model expands the meaning of liberal international reform through an appeal to Kant's notion of cosmopolitan law. The connotation that CD scholars attach to this notion exceeds the limits that have been imposed upon international politics by his statist framework. Kant did not, of course, foresee a world in which the territorially exclusive domains of formal justice that are bound up with sovereign states would be challenged by global processes.[82] Nonetheless, the CD theorists arguably revise his meaning in a way that ultimately coheres with certain less well defined elements in his thought. These elements hold that material principles of justice must also be considered when determining the boundaries of the political world. For there is a duty to alter such boundaries to gradually correspond with the purposes inherent in the inner dignity of each member of the species. It is this teleological element within Kant's thinking that potentially lends his ideological support to a reformed liberal internationalism.

CONCLUSION

In this book I have undertaken to explain two related things: first, the nature and serious limitations of Kant's commitment to international political reform; and second, the reasons why conflicting understandings of his reform project lie at the heart of contemporary divisions within liberal internationalism. In this conclusion, I make explicit the relationship between these two problems and draw together the explanations that have been developed above. In so doing, I want to emphasize the peculiar limits and possibilities of Kant's thought within the context of the crisis of liberal internationalism noted above, and the divisions among its contemporary exponents that are likely to become much more salient in the years ahead.

I have argued that any explanation of Kant's international reform project must take his theory of justice seriously, especially as it is systematically outlined in the *Metaphysics of Morals*. In chapters 1 to 3, I constructed a framework from the main elements of Kantian justice in order to explain the unique genesis, justification, and nature of his concern with international political reform. In spite of the systematic nature of his theory, its articulation as an international reform project is highly ambiguous and problematic.

In chapter 1 it was argued that Kantian subjectivity leads to a radical alienation of politics from morals, the latter of which is deemed absolutely autonomous. It is the very wide gulf between politics and morals that necessitates a political reform project in general, and reform of international politics in particular. Although moral autonomy cannot be directly manufactured within the political world, it can at the very least be preserved (and, to an ambiguous extent, promoted) if the external relations of individuals are domesticated and made compatible with morality's formal structure. Politics is made increasingly compatible with morals by making it resemble the logic of the categorical imperative via a public system of rights in which all individuals are recognized as legal ends. For Kant, such a public system of external freedom appears initially to be coeval with justice; the perfection of such justice ensures that everyone's basically negative liberty is restricted so that everyone enjoys consistent domains of freedom.

Sadly, Kant thinks that political reform requires an absolute and illimitable sovereign agent in order to secure the basic conditions of a minimally rightful condition. All reform is to be mediated through the legislative force of the sovereign, and thus the sovereign state is a prerequisite of freedom. Nevertheless, because state sovereignty is justified on the basis of its relationship to individual freedom, its moral status is rendered fundamentally suspect for two reasons. First, most generally, Kant's bifurcated vision of freedom complicates the ends to which sovereignty is alleged to contribute. As argued in chapters 2 and 3, the idea that sovereignty can be justified only by formal principles of justice is not sustained even within the context of Kant's own philosophy. This is because he draws implicitly upon the material or "moral" principle of treating humanity as an end to justify reform, thus weakening or betraying his own commitment to a politics that is concerned only with formal "legality." What this means is that sovereignty must be measured in some relation to its efficacy in promoting the cosmopolitan kingdom of ends too. But Kant himself shows that the extent to which the sovereign contributes to these moral ends is dubious, especially in the context of international politics.

Thus, the second, more specific, problem generated by Kant's view of sovereignty pertains directly to international and global politics. Although sovereigns provide the necessary conditions for freedom, they also logically negate these requirements by their mere independence from one another. In other words, their external sovereignty contradicts the formal justification of their internal sovereignty. This is because when individuals are sacrificed in interstate conflicts that necessarily arise in a state of nature, the formal and material conditions of freedom have been negated. Sovereignty is thus rendered incompatible with freedom because, in the context of international anarchy, (1) individuals have ends imposed upon them that violate their external freedom, and (2) politics requires what (Kant's own) morality expressly forbids: a systematic violation of the categorical imperative.

Kant's advocacy of international political reform is, ultimately, a complicated product of his view of justice in relation to state sovereignty. Prescriptions for international reform center upon the painful task of overcoming the contradiction between internal and external sovereignty through two related mechanisms, each of which rely upon the sovereign state's agency. The republican constitution (and a federation of such constitutions) in addition to a teleological history operate through the agency of sovereign states. In the former mechanism, states have been directly pacified by a dependence upon the desires of citizens to be free from international conflict. In tandem, several such states will, Kant hopes, form a pacific confederation, one that also realizes freedom progressively in each state. In the latter mechanism, it is the phenomenal actions of sovereigns that promote the goal of interstate peace in a long-term historical trajectory. The conflicting wills of sovereigns clash, thus "causing" a dialectic of unsocial-sociability in which individuals and states learn to calculate the necessity of rational constitutional relationships among themselves. Sovereigns are thus led to republicanism and confederation in spite of their intentions and desires.

Kant's legacy has been invoked by a wide range of contemporary liberal-minded thinkers to support international reform. This is remarkable because of the peculiar nature of Kant's justification of reform, especially the largely "illiberal" features of his doctrine of sovereignty—a doctrine that massively limits the nature and shape of reform that his texts can be said to support. But many liberal internationalists have not—mistakenly, I believe—focused sufficiently on the problematic foundations of Kant's thought. If they had, they would be in a better position to see the underlying limits and tensions of all liberal projects to simply reform interstate relations in a context of globalization. Indeed, in order to acquire a better view of the contemporary crisis of liberal internationalism, I think it is necessary to realize how Kant's problematic biases are reproduced within the tradition and how they might be supplanted.

The link between Kant's vision of international political reform and contemporary divisions within liberal internationalism is that his texts are held to contain a useful model. That is, Kant's legacy contains insights, explanations, and prescriptions to serve as guideposts for contemporary reform. But rather than a coherent "legacy," there have been competing Kantian "legacies." This is understandable because, as I have claimed, Kant's own ambiguity in his theory of justice and international reform has made his thought malleable enough for different interpretations of his meaning. These interpretations have been used in the context of competing liberal visions of the conditions needed for contemporary reformative practice. The most salient divide between liberal internationalist thinkers has been over the sovereign state and its moral and practical status in achieving reform. In my view, however, all modern attempts to render Kant's legacy into a foundation for present-day reform are potentially problematic. The problem lies not merely in the fact that such interpretations are partial or one-sided—as suggested above, perhaps the only way to build a coherent Kantian legacy is to disregard certain elements of his philosophy. Rather, it is that the different contemporary attempts to use his international thought do not adequately realize the profound limits imposed on Kant's meaning by his theory of justice. By ignoring the justificatory foundations of Kant's political thought, contemporary thinkers have read an incomplete script by an author who is, when read closely, widely out of step with the requirements of contemporary global conditions. In many ways Kant is a more appropriate model *of* the problematic and limited traditions of liberal internationalism than a model *for* its contemporary application to global politics. Any attempt to render Kant's international thought a more adequate model for future liberal internationalist theory, such as the CD model, must confront more directly the terms of his theory of justice. It is necessary to recognize the problematic role that Kant ascribes to sovereignty in achieving political reform. For although Kant's dogmatic attachment to state sovereignty does not exhaust his theory of justice, it certainly limits his vision of the nature and limits of reform in a way that parallels the problems that liberal internationalism currently faces. In the remarks that follow, I draw upon Pogge's claim that an improved Kantian politics requires above all a serious modification to his theory of justice.

Prior to the *Metaphysics of Morals*, Kant did not have a systematic position on politics. As Pogge notes, the main innovation that Kant's theory of justice adds to his critical philosophy is a conception of external duties among autonomous agents that is "argued for by appeal to pure practical reason."[1] It is thus remarkable that, given its crucial nature, so many International Relations scholars have failed to make this element of Kant's thought more central to their accounts of his international reform project. Nonetheless, although Kant's theory of justice determines the shape of his international reform project, it is not an unambiguous relationship. Although Laberge is one of the few to actually demonstrate the signal importance of the Kantian view of justice to international reform, he ultimately fails to take into account the underlying ambiguities in this vision. As I argued in chapter 2, the division between "internal" and "external" freedom is crucial to Kantian reform because it indicates how an autonomous moral realm will subordinate and inform politics. It was also noted that justice involves primarily formal principles that are abstracted from, yet resemble, the demands of the categorical imperative. In my view, Laberge wrongly insists that these formal principles of external freedom among individuals and states are the only relevant and coherent principles by which to explain Kant's international position. My conceptual framework demonstrated that Kant's theory of justice, and hence his international reform project, is actually made ambiguous because it also relies upon material principles too, ones that at first seemed to be disallowed from his framework of justice by the distinction between "legality" and "morality." The tensions within a strictly Kantian view of justice affect his position on state sovereignty. As I claimed, state sovereignty is rendered dualistic in Kant's account of international reform because there are two very distinct concepts of freedom, that is internal and external, that are employed as justification.

It is ultimately Kant's position on sovereignty that makes his thought a useful model of the liberal internationalist tradition for two reasons. Firstly, as we have seen, Kant's own ambiguity on sovereignty reflects the divisions among successive waves of liberals on the ethical adequacy of the state as an agent for international reform. His theory of justice provides not only a strong justification for the continuing centrality of the state, it also provides the grounds for a strong critique of its empirical existence. Although there are cosmopolitan claims to universal community in Kant's thought, they do not, as stated in chapter 3, suggest the necessity of weakening state sovereignty. Indeed, this restriction on cosmopolitanism to simply a moral community over and above sovereign states indicates a crucial problem with Kant's theory of justice and the reform project it inspires: Nearly everything relies upon the discretion of sovereigns. Hence, the second, and more problematic, way in which Kant's thought is a model of traditional liberal internationalism is that its dogmatic attachment to sovereignty leads to a limited vision of international reform that is prevalent in the classical and state-centric side of the tradition. Although Kant's insistence upon sovereignty is far more absolutist than subsequent liberals', it is motivated by the same excessive fears of anarchy, disorder, and global despotism, and leads to similar assumptions that international reform can proceed only through a formalistic domestication of relations among states by states. Thus the application of Kant's thought to contemporary politics may ultimately lead to a worsening of the crisis of liberal internationalism outlined above. If Kant's thought is to make a positive contribution to future attempts to articulate global reform—that is, if he is to be a model for a renewed liberal approach to global politics—we need to confront and overcome the role that sovereignty plays in his theory of justice. Pogge has articulated this strategy in a way that can, I think, be applied to international political theory; this approach coheres with the aims of the cosmopolitan democracy model.

To confront the worst defects of Kant's political legacy we need to consider why he insists upon the necessity of sovereignty. As explained in chapter 3, justice consists of a necessarily formal demand for consistent and universal domains of external freedom among individuals in society.[2] The most intolerable situation according to Kant is anarchy or lawlessness because it is the absence of any such authoritative legal system and therefore a complete negation of freedom. It is precisely the lack of enforceable determinative and authoritative judgments in society that leads Kant to endorse the sovereign in the manner that he does. Within the uncertain realm of politics, the sovereign is required because, as Pogge notes, "[p]rovisions must be made[,] through codification and adjudication, for determining definitively what the laws are, and how they apply to particular cases." For this, the sovereign is the "mechanism of authoritative determination."[3]

As argued in chapter 3, Kant's doctrine of sovereignty is an ambiguous foundation for liberal international reform. On the one hand, he suggests that any existing form of sovereignty is adequate to the goal of freedom. On the other hand, he claims that all existing sovereigns must submit to reform because they are incompatible with freedom in light of the transcendental standard of the "original contract." Kant certainly hopes that this ambivalence shall be resolved progressively through a teleological history in which sovereigns submit to (self-)reform. Kant's thought is thus the most extreme case of the classical liberal internationalist view that international reform requires a domestication of anarchy by means other than world government.

To overcome this paradoxical and crisis-ridden foundation, a modification to Kant's theory of justice is needed. Here it is important to recall that Kant relaxes his strict formalism when it comes to just international reform, as argued in chapter 3. He does so by departing from a strict usage of the domestic analogy that would have required him to advocate a world government. But Kant never drops his formalism from his vision of domestic justice. His theory of justice leads him to argue that without an absolute determinative mechanism such as the sovereign, no civil constitution or juridical state could exist.[4] Now, although other classical liberal internationalists may not all follow Kant in this "illiberal" tendency, they do share in his formalistic contractarian bias.[5] Kant was among the first thinkers to apply the analogy of autonomous individuals to the emerging world of sovereign states in the late eighteenth century.[6] In so doing, international politics became viewed "as a state of nature analogous to the one which social contract theorists presumed to have existed formerly among individuals."[7] The conviction that international politics requires domestication, rather than democratization, follows from this early liberal fear of anarchy and desire for order. Yet this desire is frustrated by the realization that such a domestication project cannot actually alter the basis of state sovereignty, at least not without risking the elimination of the inner conditions of justice and outer conditions of cultural plurality. Thus, the compromises that classical liberal internationalists have made with the sovereign state arise from their deep acceptance of the anarchy problématique as the overarching concern of politics.

There is, however, a possibility of altering Kant's theory of justice for the better in such a way that supports the reconstruction also of liberal

internationalism. Following Pogge, I noted in chapter 2 that Kant's political thought gives priority to formal over material causes. This hierarchy
is a consequence of his insistence on the absolute autonomy of the moral
realm. But, as Pogge notes, when considered fully, it appears entirely
unnecessary for Kant to assume the type of sovereign agent that he does
in order to produce a minimal condition of consistent domains of external freedom. And thus,

> A very disturbing implication of Kant's theory of justice is its demand for
> an absolute sovereign .... If we are interested in a Kantian theory of justice
> that might be acceptable today, then, it seems we shall have to modify Kant's
> own account so as to block out or mitigate that implication.[8]

There are three related reasons why this modification of Kant's own
theory would positively affect his problematic legacy to a liberal internationalism in crisis: First, it would render his thought more adequate and
relevant to the massive historical changes that have occurred since the
late eighteenth century—changes that have only accelerated with globalization. Kant's formalism might suggest that we need to hold onto
his transcendental principles of justice regardless of changing historical
circumstances like globalization. But it should be pointed out that, in
practice, today's existing juridically competent constitutional states "lack
an absolute sovereign in any comprehensible sense."[9] And thus, by Kant's
own logic, even contemporary societies are (with few exceptions) techni-
cally immobilized by life in a state of nature. In truth, modern societies
do not need such a sovereign because they have realized many of the constitutional principles that Kant assumed would evolve through struggle in
history.

Second, in removing the formal requirement for an absolute sovereign,
Kant's political thought becomes more consistent with itself and with
modern liberalism. As Pogge notes, not only would civil disobedience and
conscientious refusal now be permitted, for example, by Kantian politics,
but an authentic separation of powers would become possible. Kant's
much desired goals of a republican state and confederal international
system are actually thwarted by the permanent reserve of "emergency"
powers that he allows for the sovereign. Again, such a redescription of
Kant's thought means that we relax even further the priority of formal
over material causes in his theory of justice. If his excessive formalism is
rejected, his weak "surrogate" confederation of sovereign states for international justice begins to lose its appeal—and cosmopolitical democracy
becomes more plausible. Without a dogmatic view of sovereignty, Kant's
model would "come closer to [his own] republican ideal insofar as world

law would reflect democratic procedures rather than the distribution of power among governments."[10]

Finally, Kant's political and international theory would begin to enable, rather than impede, the realization of enlightenment that he claims to advocate. Kant frequently invokes the existence of important material purposes within politics that he hopes will be realized one day. But his anachronism concerning sovereignty and the formalism that has supported it have unnecessarily subordinated these purposes. It is long past the time when it is adequate to merely hope, with Kant, that these ethico-political purposes can be accommodated by the discretionary will of sovereign states. By removing the absolute and problematic connection that the sovereignty symbol has been given with freedom and justice in Kant's thought, we would be better equipped to actually practice rather than simply hope for enlightenment. For present-day liberals, this would mean embracing more direct cosmopolitan means to promote individual autonomy and justice.

NOTES

INTRODUCTION

1. Stanley Hoffmann, "The Crisis of Liberal Internationalism," *Foreign Policy* 98 (1995): 159–177. See also James L. Richardson, *Contending Liberalisms in World Politics: Ideology and Power* (Boulder: Lynne Rienner Publishers, 2001).

2. Charles W. Kegley Jr., "The Neoliberal Challenge to Realist Theories of World Politics: An Introduction," in *Controversies in International Politics: Realism and the Neoliberal Challenge*, ed. Charles W. Kegley Jr. (New York: St. Martin's Press, 1995), 1–14; Bruce Russett, *Grasping the Democratic Peace: Principles of a Post-Cold War World* (Princeton: Princeton University Press, 1993).

3. Samuel P. Huntington, *The Third Wave: Democratization in the Late Twentieth Century* (Norman: University of Oklahoma Press, 1991); Bruce Russett, *Grasping the Democratic Peace*. For a critical view on the promotion of democracy after the Cold War, see William I. Robinson, *Promoting Polyarchy: Globalization, US Intervention and Hegemony* (Cambridge: Cambridge University Press, 1998).

4. James N. Rosenau, *Along the Domestic-Foreign Frontier: Exploring Governance in a Turbulent World* (Cambridge: Cambridge University Press, 1997).

5. Richard Devetak and Richard Higgott, "Justice Unbound? Globalization, States, and the Transformation of the Social Bond," *International Affairs* 75, 3 (1999): 485; Richard Falk, "The Pursuit of International Justice: Present Dilemmas and an Imagined Future," *Journal of International Affairs* 52, 2 (1999): 421.

6. Francis Fukuyama, *The End of History and the Last Man* (New York: Avon Books, 1992).

7. Andrew Moravcsik, "Taking Preferences Seriously: A Liberal Theory of International Politics," *International Organization* 51, 4 (1997): 513–553.

8. Richardson, *Contending Liberalisms;* David Long, "Conclusion: Inter-War Idealism, Liberal Internationalism, and Contemporary International Theory," in *Thinkers of the Twenty Years' Crisis*, eds. David Long and Peter Wilson (Oxford: Clarendon Press, 1995), 302–328; Michael W. Doyle, *Ways of War and Peace: Realism, Liberalism, Socialism* (New York: W. W. Norton and Company, 1997).

9. Long, "Conclusion," 302–328. Brian C. Schmidt, *The Political Discourse of Anarchy: A Disciplinary History of International Relations* (Albany: State University of New York Press, 1998).

10. On this theme, see Mark F. N. Franke, *Global Limits: Immanuel Kant, International Relations, and Critique in World Politics* (Albany: State University of New York Press, 2001), 2.
11. Cf. Kimberly Hutchings, *Kant, Critique and Politics* (London: Routledge, 1996).
12. In this respect, I am less convinced than Georg Cavallar about the extent to which Kantian antinomies and dichotomies are resolved in the realm of politics and practical reason. See his *Kant and the Theory and Practice of International Right* (Cardiff: University of Wales Press, 1999).
13. See in particular David Held, *Democracy and the Global Order: From the Modern State to Cosmopolitan Governance* (Stanford: Stanford University Press, 1995), and Daniele Archibugi, "Cosmopolital Democracy," *New Left Review* second series, 4 (2000): 137–150.
14. This has been a tendency of members of the so-called English School. See Martin Wight, *International Theory: The Three Traditions* (London: Leicester University Press, 1991); Hedley Bull, *The Anarchical Society: A Study of Order in World Politics* (London: Macmillan, 1977).
15. Thomas W. Pogge, "Kant's Theory of Justice," *Kant-Studien* 79, 4 (1988): 407–408.
16. Pierre Laberge, "Kant on Justice and the Law of Nations," in *International Society: Diverse Ethical Perspectives,* ed. David R. Mapel and Terry Nardin (Princeton: Princeton University Press, 1998), 83–102.
17. The "dogma" of sovereignty is Pogge's phrase, "Kant's Theory of Justice," 431–433; Thomas W. Pogge, "Cosmopolitanism and Sovereignty," *Ethics* 103, 1 (1992): 50; and Thomas W. Pogge, *Realizing Rawls* (Ithaca: Cornell University Press, 1989), 216. Cf. Cavallar, *Kant and the Theory,* 57.
18. Fernando R. Tesón, "Kantian International Liberalism," in *International Society: Diverse Ethical Perspectives,* ed., David R. Mapel and Terry Nardin (Princeton: Princeton University Press, 1998), 103.

CHAPTER 1   THE FOUNDATIONS OF KANT'S REFORM PROJECT: POLITICS AND MORALS

1. C.Pr, 162/169.
2. The "rights of man" is no doubt a predecessor to more recent notions of human rights. However, it is appropriate because Kant's writings are contemporaneous to—and generally sympathetic with—the aims of the French Revolution. Regrettably, references to Kant's political discourse require the quotation of his gendered vocabulary.
3. Jean-Jacques Rousseau, *The First and Second Discourses,* ed. Roger D. Masters, trans. Roger D. Masters and Judith R. Masters (New York: St. Martin's Press, 1964).
4. Susan Meld Shell, "Kant's Political Cosmology: Freedom and Desire in the 'Remarks' Concerning *Observations on the Feeling of the Beautiful and the*

Sublime," in *Essays on Kant's Political Philosophy,* ed. Howard Williams (Cardiff: University of Wales Press, 1992), 81.

5. Susan Meld Shell, *The Rights of Reason: A Study of Kant's Philosophy and Politics* (Toronto: University of Toronto Press, 1980), 21. See also Richard L. Velkey, *Freedom and the Ends of Reason: On the Moral Foundation of Kant's Critical Philosophy* (Chicago: University of Chicago Press, 1989), 6–8.

6. As George Armstrong Kelley writes, Kant "withdraws from the bombardment of Rousseau's moralism, while accepting his insights on freedom," in Kelley, *Idealism, Politics and History: Sources of Hegelian Thought* (Cambridge: Cambridge University Press, 1969), 99.

7. C.Pur, Bxxv/27.

8. See Aristotle, *The Ethics* (Toronto: Penguin Books, 1993), 203–225; cf. GMM, 391/60.

9. C.Pr, 15/15.

10. On Kant's use of political and legal metaphors in the first *Critique*, see Hutchings, *Kant, Critique and Politics* (London: Routledge, 1996), 1–37, and Onora O'Neill, *Constructions of Reason* (Cambridge: Cambridge University Press, 1989).

11. C.Pur, Bxxx/31.

12. Cf. Hobbes, *Leviathan* (Toronto: Penguin Books, 1986), 118–121.

13. Shell, *Rights of Reason,* 11.

14. See GMM, 395/62–3; CBH, 226.

15. Shell, *Rights of Reason,* 3.

16. See Hobbes, *Leviathan,* 82f., 119, 183ff.

17. Joseph Knippenberg, "The Politics of Kant's Philosophy," in *Kant and Political Philosophy: the Contemporary Legacy,* ed. Ronald Beiner and William James Booth (New Haven: Yale University Press, 1993), 157.

18. See Shell, *The Rights of Reason,* 4.

19. C.Pur, Bxvii–xviii/21–22.

20. C.Pur, Bxx/24.

21. As Otfried Höffe notes, "Kant's revolution ... enables human reason [to] liberate itself from the biases of the natural perspective, epistemological realism," in Höffe, *Immanuel Kant,* trans. Marshall Farrier (Albany: State University of New York Press, 1994), 38.

22. C.Pur, Bxxvi/28.

23. C.Pur, A709 = B737/665.

24. William James Booth, *Interpreting the World: Kant's Philosophy of History and Politics* (Toronto: University of Toronto Press, 1986), 17.

25. GMM, 389/57, 431/98; C.Pr, 33/33.

26. C.Pur, Bxxix/30–1; C.Pr, 4/4; GMM, 456/123–4; MM, 220/14.

27. C.Pr, 6n/6.

28. The other regulative Ideas that Kant mentions in this context are God and the immortality of the soul, C.Pur, Bxxxii–xxxxiii/28–9. Cf. C.Pr, 4/4, 114–134/ 120–140.

29. Niccolò Machiavelli, *The Prince,* trans. Harvey C. Mansfield Jr. (Chicago: University of Chicago Press, 1985), 61–62.

30. PP, 116–125.
31. PP, 125.
32. GMM, 437/105.
33. GMM, 428/96.
34. GMM, 392/60.
35. GMM, 435/102.
36. See Hobbes, *Leviathan,* 95–99.
37. C.Pr, 34/34.
38. See GMM, 389/57.
39. GMM, 407/75.
40. Machiavelli, *The Prince,* 61.
41. C.Pr, 26/27.
42. C.Pr, 21/19.
43. GMM, 389/56.
44. GMM, 408/75.
45. UH, 46.
46. GMM, 389/57.
47. GMM, 412/80.
48. Cf. Aristotle, *The Politics,* trans. T. A. Sinclair (Toronto: Penguin Books, 1992), 61.
49. See GMM, 426/93.
50. See MM, 380/146, 397/158.
51. CBH, 226.
52. Machiavelli, *The Prince,* passim.
53. GMM, 408/75.

Chapter 2   The Ethico-Political Ambiguity of Kantian Freedom

1. C.Pr, 3/3.
2. Isaiah Berlin, *Four Essays on Liberty* (Oxford: Oxford University Press, 1969), 121, 131.
3. See for example John Gray, "Introduction," in *Conceptions of Liberty in Political Philosophy,* ed. Zbigniew Pelczynski and John Gray (London: The Athlone Press, 1984), 5.
4. Berlin, *Four Essays on Liberty,* 131.
5. Ibid., 135–136.
6. Elie Kedourie, *Nationalism,* 4th ed. (Oxford: Basil Blackwell, 1993), 14–17.
7. Although Berlin admits to important expressions of negative freedom in Kant's thought, he denies their importance by suggesting that they are exceptional deviations from, rather than fundamental to, Kant's politics; *Four Essays on Liberty,* 153n. Kedourie refuses to consider that self-legislation or autonomy is but one aspect of Kant's thought on freedom that coexists with statements that resemble a more "classical" liberalism; *Nationalism,* 137.
8. Howard Williams, *Kant's Political Philosophy* (Oxford: Basil Blackwell, 1983), 68.
9. Ibid., vii.

10. Otfried Höffe, *Immanuel Kant,* trans. Marshall Farrier (Albany: State University of New York Press, 1994), 174; see also Otfried Höffe, "Even a Nation of Devils Needs the State: the Dilemma of Natural Justice," in *Essays on Kant's Political Philosophy,* ed. Howard Williams (Cardiff: University of Wales Press, 1992), 128.

11. See Charles Taylor, "Kant's Theory of Freedom," in *Conceptions of Liberty in Political Philosophy,* ed. Pelczynski and Gray, 100–122.

12. Ibid., 114.

13. Ibid., 108.

14. See Thomas W. Pogge, "Kant's Theory of Justice," *Kant-Studien* 79, 4 (1988): 409f.

15. C.Pr, 28/28, emphasis added.

16. MM, 406–7/165.

17. GMM, 455/123.

18. Again these terms bear a surface resemblance to those used by Berlin. Few have done more to clarify the different ways in which Kant speaks of freedom than Lewis White Beck, "Kant's Two Concepts of the Will in Their Political Context," in *Kant and Political Philosophy,* ed. Ronald Beiner and William James Booth (New Haven: Yale University Press, 1993), 38–49. Beck notes that Kant switches back and forth, often inconsistently, between two distinct connotations of the same word. However, Kant is most consistent when he uses two different words—*Wille* and *Willkür*—that refer to two senses of inner freedom. See GMM, 445/114 and 452–3/120; cf. C.Pur, A553–4 = B589/549.

19. C.Pr, 33/33–34.

20. C.Pr, 29/29.

21. GMM, 409/76.

22. See MM, 214/13.

23. Bernard Carnois, *The Coherence of Kant's Doctrine of Freedom,* trans. David Booth (Chicago: University of Chicago Press, 1987), 47.

24. GMM, 434/101.

25. GMM, 431/98, emphasis in original; see also TP, 64.

26. GMM, 403/71; see also MM, 375/141.

27. C.Pr, 64/67, emphasis added for the sake of clarity.

28. GMM, 402/70, emphasis in original.

29. G. W. F. Hegel, *The Philosophy of Right,* trans. T. M. Knox (Oxford: Oxford University Press, 1967), 89.

30. MM, 237/30.

31. GMM, 435/102.

32. Höffe, *Kant,* 137; also William Galston, "What Is Living and What Is Dead in Kant's Practical Philosophy," in *Kant and Political Philosophy,* ed. Ronald Beiner and William James Booth (New Haven: Yale University Press, 1993), 214.

33. Leslie Arthur Mulholland, *Kant's System of Rights* (New York: Columbia University Press, 1990), 3.

34. MM, 216/10.

35. PP, 125.

36. PP, 121–122.

37. TP, 86.
38. Pogge, "Kant's Theory of Justice," 409.
39. MM, 316/93.
40. Allen D. Rosen, *Kant's Theory of Justice* (Ithaca: Cornell University Press, 1993), 10; see MM, 312/89–90.
41. MM, 237/30.
42. Rosen, *Kant's Theory of Justice,* 12–13.
43. MM, 230/24; cf. PP, 99.
44. MM, 230/24.
45. See Pierre Laberge, "Kant on Justice and the Law of Nations," in *International Society: Diverse Ethical Perspectives,* ed. David R. Mapel and Terry Nardin (Princeton: Princeton University Press, 1998), 87.
46. MM, 313/90; TP, 77–79.
47. MM, 223/16, 313–315/90–93; TP, 78–79. For Rousseau's formulation of freedom, see *The Social Contract,* trans. G. D. H. Cole (London: Everyman's Library, 1986), 195–196.
48. MM, 316/93.
49. GMM, 431/98; C.Pr, 33/33–34.
50. Taylor, "Kant's Theory of Freedom," 110.
51. C.Pr, 72/75.
52. MM, 220/21.
53. MM, 219/20.
54. MM, 231/25.
55. Höffe, *Kant,* 171.
56. MM, 230/23–24.
57. MM, 381/146.
58. MM, 233/26.
59. PP, 116.
60. Pogge, "Kant's Theory of Justice," 409.
61. Ibid., 411.
62. C.Pr, 76/79.
63. Rosen, "Kant's Theory of Justice," 43.
64. C.Pr, 152/158.
65. UH, 46.
66. Patrick Riley, "Elements of Kant's Practical Philosophy," in *Kant and Political Philosophy,* ed. Ronald Beiner and William James Booth (New Haven: Yale University Press, 1993), 20.
67. C.Pr, 70–71/74.
68. Riley, "Elements of Kant's Practical Philosophy," 11.
69. This reading of Kant is present in the work of Laberge and Höffe. See Laberge, "Kant on Justice and the Law of Nations"; Höffe, *Kant,* passim.
70. Pogge, "Kant's Theory of Justice."
71. Ibid., 413.
72. UH, 44–45.
73. Galston, "What Is Living and What Is Dead," 216, 220.

CHAPTER 3   KANT, STATE SOVEREIGNTY, AND INTERNATIONAL REFORM

1. Patrick Riley, *Kant's Political Philosophy* (Totowa, NJ: Rowman and Littlefield, 1983), 117.
2. Jens Bartelson, *A Genealogy of Sovereignty* (Cambridge: Cambridge University Press, 1995), 214.
3. As Pierre Laberge suggests, this would make Kant's international thought much closer or consistent with the English School vision of world politics than is assumed by Martin Wight and Hedley Bull. See Laberge, "Kant on Justice and the Law of Nations," in *International Society: Diverse Ethical Perspectives,* ed. David R. Mapel and Terry Nardin (Princeton: Princeton University Press, 1998), 82.
4. F. H. Hinsley, *Sovereignty,* 2nd ed. (Cambridge: Cambridge University Press, 1986), 158. Cf. Hedley Bull, *The Anarchical Society: A Study of Order in World Politics* (London: Macmillan, 1977), 8.
5. Bartelson places this distinction within a specific historical context. See Bartelson, *A Genealogy of Sovereignty,* passim.
6. Cf. Quentin Skinner, "Meaning and Understanding in the History of Ideas," in *Meaning and Context: Quentin Skinner and His Critics,* ed. James Tully (Cambridge, UK: Polity Press, 1988), 34–35.
7. MM, 276/64–341/112.
8. UH, 46.
9. TP, 73.
10. UH, 46.
11. UH, 46.
12. MM, 312/89; TP, 71–2; cf. GMM, 389/57.
13. MM, 312/89–90.
14. MM, 237/30.
15. MM, 307/89; cf. TP, 73.
16. MM, 320/96–7; TP, 81. See Peter Nicholson, "Kant on the Duty Never to Resist the Sovereign," *Ethics* 86, 3 (1976): 214–230.
17. See MM, 230–231/24; TP, 75; PP, 99; UH, 46–47.
18. This questioning is wrong if it undermines the sovereign, the ultimate judge of what is a threat. Of course, Kant attempts to assure his contemporary sovereign that the public use of reason and criticism is not a threat to the foundations of political order; see QE, 54–60.
19. MM, 319/95.
20. See Pogge for the charge of "dogmatism," in "Kant's Theory of Justice," *Kant-Studien* 79, 4 (1988): 431–433, and Pogge, "Cosmopolitanism and Sovereignty," *Ethics* 103, 1 (1992): 59. As Rosen notes, there is an incompatibility between Kant's absolutist statements on sovereignty and his subsequent demand that states be republican (i.e., divided constitutionally), *Kant's Theory of Justice* (Ithaca: Cornell University Press, 1993), 143–144.

21. MM, 317/94; TP, 75. Cf. Hobbes, *Leviathan* (Toronto: Penguin Books, 1986), 313. For an argument concerning Hobbesian ideas in Kant's philosophy, see Richard Tuck, *The Rights of Reason: Political Thought and International Order from Grotius to Kant* (Oxford: Oxford University Press, 1999), 207–225.

22. CF, 182–183.

23. MM, 371/136.

24. See MM, 216/10.

25. Nicholson, "Kant on the Duty," 223.

26. PP, 118n.

27. CF, 185; I am using Riley's slightly altered translation of this paragraph, in "Elements of Kant's Political Philosophy," in *Kant and Political Philosophy,* ed. Ronald Beiner and William James Booth (New Haven: Yale University Press, 1993), 20. See also MM, 345/115–116.

28. PP, 113.

29. MM, 340/112; TP, 79; cf. CF, 187.

30. MM, 340/112.

31. MM, 345/115.

32. In this definition, the sovereign is the only judge "competent to render a verdict having rightful force," MM, 312/90.

33. Nicholson, "Kant on the Duty," 218.

34. MM, 314/91.

35. Cavallar argues that Kant's absolutist vision of sovereignty is displaced by a "new" paradigm of "popular sovereignty," Cavallar, *Kant and the Theory and Practice of International Right* (Cardiff: University of Wales Press, 1999), 58. However, I think this displacement appears incomplete—Kant does not explicitly repudiate or alter his dogmatic statements about sovereignty that clearly undercut the popular (or potentially democratic) foundations of legislative authority.

36. MM, 321–322/98. See Williams, *Kant's Political Philosophy* (Oxford: Basil Blackwell, 1993), ix.

37. MM, 307/85.

38. TP, 80–81.

39. Thomas W. Pogge, "Is Kant's *Rechtslehre* Comprehensive?" *The Southern Journal of Philosophy* 36, Supplement (1997): 177.

40. See for example Laberge, "Kant on Justice and the Law of Nations."

41. PP, 94–5.

42. Martin Wight, "Why Is There No International Theory?" in *Diplomatic Investigations,* ed. Herbert Butterfield and Martin Wight (London: George Allen & Unwin, 1966), 21–28. Cf. F. H. Hinsley, *Power and the Pursuit of Peace: Theory and Practice in the History of Relations Among States* (Cambridge: Cambridge University Press, 1963), 6.

43. Ibid.

44. See Kant's statements about the positive role of linguistic and religious differences in frustrating any potential global despotism, PP, 113–114.

45. PP, 103.

46. TP, 73.

47. The idea of the "domestic analogy" is analyzed with care in Hidemi Suganami, "Reflections on the Domestic Analogy: The Case of Bull, Beitz and Linklater," *Review of International Studies* 12, 2 (1986): 145–158, and Hidemi Suganami, *The Domestic Analogy in World Order Proposals* (Cambridge: Cambridge University Press, 1989).

48. Laberge, "Kant on Justice and the Law of Nations," 90.

49. Pogge, "Kant's Theory of Justice," 428.

50. UH, 47, emphasis removed.

51. PP, 94–95.

52. MM, 345/116.

53. UH, 47, 51.

54. See for example Carl Joachim Friedrich, *Inevitable Peace* (Cambridge: Harvard University Press, 1948), 30–33.

55. Laberge, "Kant on Justice and the Law of Nations," 93.

56. The second preliminary article is worth quoting: "No independently existing state, whether it be large or small, may be acquired by another state by inheritance, exchange, purchase or gift," PP, 94. The fifth preliminary article, too, is important: "No state shall forcibly interfere in the constitution and government of another state," PP, 96.

57. Nicholas Greenwood Onuf, *The Republican Legacy in International Thought* (Cambridge: Cambridge University Press, 1998).

58. See Michael W. Doyle, *Ways of War and Peace: Realism, Liberalism and Socialism* (New York: W. W. Norton & Company, 1997), 205–206.

59. PP, 100.

60. PP, 100.

61. PP, 101.

62. Kant's vision of citizenship includes only "active" or independent members of society, that is, those who are free from an economic (or other kinds of) dependency upon others. Nevertheless, he holds that all "subjects" of the state should be granted legal "equality"; see TP, 74–77.

63. TP, 79.

64. TP, 79; PP, 100.

65. PP, 102; cf. MM, 343/114.

66. Hinsley, *Power and the Pursuit of Peace,* 66.

67. PP, 117.

68. MM, 312/89–90.

69. PP, 105.

70. PP, 102.

71. MM, 344–345/114–115.

72. PP, 104.

73. TP, 90–91; PP, 113–114; MM, 350/119.

74. UH, 47.

75. TP, 79.

76. PP, 104–105.

77. PP, 102; MM, 343/114. See also REL, 89n.
78. PP, 98, emphasis added to "guarantee"; cf. MM, 350/119.
79. MM, 349/118–119.
80. Hannah Arendt, *Lectures on Kant's Political Philosophy*, ed. Ronald Beiner (Chicago: University of Chicago Press, 1982), 14. See also Williams, *Kant's Political Philosophy*, 2.
81. UH, 41.
82. UH, 52, emphasis added.
83. UH, 42
84. PP, 109; cf. CF, 177.
85. UH, 44.
86. UH, 46.
87. PP, 112–113.
88. Laberge, "Kant on Justice and the Law of Nations," 98.
89. UH, 47.
90. TP, 90.
91. PP, 107; cf. MM, 352/121. This quotation certainly evokes Kant's moral cosmopolitanism. But it might be objected that I have not sufficiently considered the contents of his third definitive article in my analysis of the two mechanisms for international reform, that is, cosmopolitan law. It should be recalled that nowhere does Kant indicate that the definitive articles correspond to clear and distinct mechanisms.

CHAPTER 4   LIBERAL INTERNATIONALISM AND THE KANTIAN "LEGACY"

1. Richard Tuck, *The Rights of War and Peace: Political Thought and International Order From Grotius to Kant* (Oxford: Oxford University Press, 1999), 229–230.
2. On the renaissance of liberal perspectives in International Relations, see Richard A. Matthew and Mark W. Zacher, "Liberal International Theory: Common Threads, Divergent Strands," in *Controversies in International Politics: Realism and the Neoliberal Challenge*, ed. Charles W. Kegley Jr. (New York: St. Martin's Press, 1995), 107–150; Peter Wilson, "Introduction," in *Thinkers of the Twenty Years' Crisis: Inter-War Idealism Reassessed*, ed. David Long and Peter Wilson (Oxford: Clarendon Press, 1995), 2–14; and Kegley, "The Neoliberal Challenge," in *Controversies in International Politics*, ed. Kegley, 1–14.
3. See for example Bruce Russett, *Grasping the Democratic Peace: Principles of a Post-Cold War World* (Princeton: Princeton University Press, 1993), 24. See also the debates in David A. Baldwin, ed., *Neorealism and Neoliberalism: The Contemporary Debate* (New York: Columbia University Press, 1993); and Sean M. Lynn-Jones and Steven E. Miller, eds., *Debating the Democratic Peace* (Cambridge: MIT Press, 1996).
4. Michael W. Doyle, *Ways of War and Peace: Realism, Liberalism and Socialism* (New York: W. W. Norton & Company, 1997), 206.

5. This discussion of the nature of liberalism is necessarily truncated because the present book aims only to establish its interrelation with internationalism. For larger studies of liberalism, see John Gray, *Liberalism*, 2nd ed. (Minneapolis: University of Minnesota Press, 1995), 56–8; and James Meadowcroft, ed., *The Liberal Political Tradition: Contemporary Reappraisals* (Cheltenham, UK: Edward Elgar, 1996), 4.

6. Isaiah Berlin, *Four Essays on Liberty* (Oxford: Oxford University Press, 1969), also some of the contributions to Zbigniew Pelczynski and John Gray, eds., *Conceptions of Liberty in Political Philosophy* (London: The Athlone Press, 1984).

7. Fred Halliday, "Three Concepts of Internationalism," *International Affairs* 64, 2 (1988): 188.

8. Ibid.

9. Ibid., 194–195. Halliday describes two other strands of internationalism, "hegemonic" and "revolutionary." The former is "an extension of nationalism" because, in identifying the interests of all nations with its own, hegemonic internationalism subordinates other states in the international system to its own vision. Revolutionary internationalism is the exporting of the principles that have radically reshaped one particular society to others, the best examples of which are the French Revolution and, much more recently, Iran's Islamic revolution. A problem that arises is not merely that there are at least these three varieties of internationalism but also—which Halliday does not seem to consider—that they may overlap. States that have been animated by liberal principles, such as Great Britain and the United States, have frequently been hegemonic in orientation, and revolutionary states such as France have been associated with the principles of liberalism.

10. Ibid., 188.

11. Suganami, *The Domestic Analogy in World Order Proposals* (Cambridge: Cambridge University Press, 1989), 1–6.

12. Hoffmann, "The Crisis of Liberal Internationalism," *Foreign Policy* 98 (1995): 161.

13. E. H. Carr, *The Twenty Years' Crisis* (Edinburgh: R&R Clark, 1942), 43–80.

14. This term is borrowed from Robert W. Cox, "Social Forces, States, and World Orders: Beyond International Relations Theory," in *Neorealism and Its Critics*, ed. Robert O. Keohane (New York: Columbia University Press, 1986), 208.

15. Kjell Goldmann, *The Logic of Internationalism: Coercion and Accommodation* (London: Routledge, 1994), x.

16. Ibid., 1.

17. Although freedom is held to be crucial to understanding the specifically liberal origins and character of this approach to politics, its realization does not seem to have any obvious or inherent connection to the mechanisms fulfilling the internationalist agenda. See for example Doyle, "Kant, Liberal Legacies and Foreign Affairs," in *Debating the Democratic Peace,* ed. Michael E. Brown, Sean M. Lynn-Jones and Steven E. Miller (Cambridge: MIT Press, 1996), 3–53; Doyle, *Ways of War and Peace,* 204; Robert O. Keohane, "International Liberalism Reconsidered," in *The Economic Limits to Modern Politics,* ed.

John Dunn (Cambridge: Cambridge University Press, 1990), 165–194; and
to a limited extent Matthew and Zacher, "Liberal International Theory."
Cf. Stanley Hoffmann, *Janus and Minerva: Essays on the Theory and Practice of
International Politics* (Boulder: Westview Press, 1987), 395.

18. Goldmann conceives of liberal internationalism in pragmatic, nonfounda-
tional terms. And yet he acknowledges that the reform mechanisms he
discusses are derived from "the liberal tradition of international ethics";
The Logic of Internationalism, xiii.

19. John Sylvester Hemleben, *Plans for World Peace through Six Centuries*
(New York: Garland Publishing Company, 1943); F. H. Hinsley, *Power and the
Pursuit of Peace: Theory and Practice in the History of Relations Among States*
(Cambridge: Cambridge University Press, 1963); and Daniele Archibugi,
"Models of International Organization in Perpetual Peace Projects," *Review of
International Studies* 18, 4 (1992): 295–317.

20. John Locke, *Second Treatise of Government* (Indianapolis: Hackett Publishing
Company, 1980), chaps. 1–3, and esp. 8.

21. Doyle, *Ways of War and Peace*, 226; see also Michael Joseph Smith, "Liberalism
and International Reform," in *Traditions of International Ethics*, ed. Terry Nardin
and David R. Mapel (Cambridge: Cambridge University Press, 1992), 203.

22. Hinsley, *Power and the Pursuit of Peace*, 33.

23. Doyle, *Ways of War and Peace*, 230.

24. Ibid., 233–234.

25. Ibid.

26. Of course, many liberals have suspended this principle when discussing non-
European peoples. See, in the case of Woodrow Wilson, Cynthia Weber,
Simulating Sovereignty: Intervention, the State, and Symbolic Exchange
(Cambridge: Cambridge University Press, 1995), chap. 5.

27. Inis L. Claude Jr., *Swords into Plowshares: The Problems and Progress of
International Organization*, 4th ed. (New York: Random House, 1984), 51ff.,
and Smith, "Liberalism and International Reform," 215.

28. Francis Fukuyama, *The End of History and the Last Man*; also Russett,
Grasping the Democratic Peace.

29. Michael Freeden, *New Liberalism: An Ideology of Social Reform* (Oxford:
Clarendon Press, 1978).

30. David Long, "The Harvard School of Liberal International Theory: A Case for
Closure," *Millennium: Journal of International Studies* 24, 3 (1995): 502.

31. Smith, "Liberalism and International Reform," 220.

32. David Long, "Conclusion: Inter-War Idealism, Liberal Internationalism, and
Contemporary International Theory," in *Thinkers of the Twenty Years' Crisis:
Inter-War Idealism Reassessed*, ed. David Long and Peter Wilson (Oxford:
Clarendon Press, 1995), 313.

33. David Mitrany, *A Working Peace System* (Chicago: Quadrangle Books, 1966).

34. Ernst B. Haas, *Beyond the Nation-State* (Stanford: Stanford University Press,
1964).

35. Charles Pentland, *Integration Theory and European Integration* (London: Faber
and Faber, 1973), 70, 81; see also the contributions to Lucian M. Ashworth

and David Long, eds., *New Perspectives on International Functionalism* (Basingstoke, UK: Macmillan, 1999).

36. Pentland, *Integration Theory and European Integration*, 81, emphasis added.
37. For example, Doyle's entire discussion of the liberal tradition omits mention of nonstatist liberals in *Ways of War and Peace*.
38. Locke, *Second Treatise of Government*, chap. 14. It should be recalled from my previous chapter that Kant's doctrine of sovereignty contains decidedly illiberal sentiments toward the rights of rebellion when compared to Locke.
39. For example PP, 104–105 and 129.
40. Hoffmann, "The Crisis of Liberal Internationalism," 164.
41. Doyle, "Kant, Liberal Legacies and Foreign Affairs," 10.
42. PP, 103.
43. Kant's critique of democracy can also be read as a critique of popular sovereignty as a sufficient condition of peace; PP, 100–101. This will be discussed further in chapter 6.
44. Richardson, "Contending Liberalisms: Past and Present," *European Journal of International Relations* 3, 1 (1997): 17.
45. See Mitrany's reflections on international organizations in *A Working Peace System*, 149–156.
46. Hoffmann, "The Crisis of Liberal Internationalism," 163.
47. Smith, "Liberalism and International Reform," 212.
48. The fourth preliminary article requires that states abolish all national debts; PP, 95.
49. Whether these constitutions can be properly called democratic in the case of Kant, as some contemporary liberal theorists claim, shall be discussed in chapter 6 below.
50. David Held, "Cosmopolitan Democracy and the Global Order: Reflections on the 200th Anniversary of Kant's 'Perpetual Peace,'" *Alternatives* 20, 4 (1995): 415–429; Daniele Archibugi, "Immanuel Kant, Cosmopolitan Law and Peace," *European Journal of International Relations* 1, 4 (1995): 429–456.
51. Jens Bartelson, "The Trial of Judgment: A Note on Kant and the Paradoxes of Internationalism," *International Studies Quarterly* 39, 2 (1995): 256–257.
52. R. B. J. Walker, *Inside/Outside: International Relations as Political Theory* (Cambridge: Cambridge University Press, 1993), 161.
53. Jack S. Levy, "Domestic Politics and War," in *The Origin and Prevention of Major Wars*, ed. R. I. Rotberg and T. K. Rabb (Cambridge: Cambridge University Press, 1989), 88.
54. Doyle, "Kant, Liberal Legacies and Foreign Affairs," 30.
55. Chris Brown, "'Really Existing Liberalism' and International Order," *Millennium: Journal of International Studies* 21, 3 (1992): 313–328.
56. Andrew Linklater, *Men and Citizens in the Theory of International Relations* (London: Macmillan, 1982), 11; see also Linklater, *Beyond Realism and Marxism: Critical Theory and International Relations* (London: Macmillan, 1990); Linklater, "The Problem of Community in International Relations," *Alternatives* 15, 2 (1990): 135–153; Linklater, "Citizenship and Sovereignty in the Post-Westphalian State," *European Journal of International Relations* 2,

1 (1996): 77–103; and Linklater, *The Transformation of Community: the Ethical Foundations of the Post-Westphalian Era* (Cambridge, UK: Polity Press, 1998), 220.

It might be objected that Linklater's scholarly career does not support liberal internationalism, given his use of Hegelian and Marxist-inspired critical theory. But critical theory need not be incompatible with the essential goals of liberal internationalism. We must take Linklater's own statement of intent seriously: "The specific contribution that critical theory can make to the next stage of international relations theory starts from the premise that the emancipatory project ought to be more central to the field. Critical theory presents the case for *recovering the old idealist program,* modernized to take account of the various intellectual developments and debates which have shaped the field over the past sixty or seventy years," in "The Question of the Next Stage in International Relations: A Critical-Theoretical Point of View," *Millennium: Journal of International Studies* 21, 1 (1992): 98, emphasis added. Cf. Beate Jahn, "One Step Forward, Two Steps Back: Critical Theory as the Latest Edition of Liberal Idealism," *Millennium* 27, 3 (1998): 613–641.

57. Linklater, *Men and Citizens,* xi.
58. Ibid., 11.
59. Ibid., 99.
60. Ibid.
61. Ibid., 116.
62. Ibid., 114; see also 99.
63. Ibid., 115–116.
64. Bartelson, "The Trial of Judgment," 264.

CHAPTER 5   THE CRISIS OF LIBERAL INTERNATIONALISM:
FROM INTERNATIONAL TO GLOBAL GOVERNING
INSTITUTIONS

1. Pierre Hassner, "Beyond Nationalism and Internationalism: Ethnicity and World Order," *Survival* 35, 2 (1993): 53.
2. Stanley Hoffmann, "The Crisis of Liberal Internationalism," *Foreign Policy* 98 (1995): 159–177.
3. For an example, see the remarks of Canada's former minister of foreign affairs, Lloyd Axworthy: "Kosovo and the Human Security Agenda," Notes for an Address by the Honorable Lloyd Axworthy to the Woodrow Wilson School of Public and International Relations, Princeton University, April 7, 1999, 2.
4. Tim Judah, *Kosovo: War and Revenge* (New York: Yale University Press, 2000).
5. "Seattle Comes to Washington," *The Economist,* April 15, 2000; "Clueless in Seattle," *The Economist,* December 4, 1999, 17; "The Battle in Seattle," *The Economist,* November 27, 1999. See also Robert O'Brien, Anne Marie Goetz, Jan Aart Scholte, and Marc Williams, eds., *Contesting Global*

Governance: Multilateral Economic Institutions and Global Social Movements (Cambridge: Cambridge University Press, 2000).

6. For Hoffmann's self-description as a "liberal," see *Janus and Minerva: Essays on the Theory and Practice of International Politics* (Boulder: Westview Press, 1987), 395; also his *Duties Beyond Borders: On the Limits and Possibilities of Ethical International Politics* (Syracuse, NY: Syracuse University Press, 1981), 8–10.

7. Hoffmann, "The Crisis of Liberal Internationalism," 167.

8. Cf. Linklater, *The Transformation of Community: the Ethical Foundations of the Post-Westphalian Era* (Cambridge, UK: Polity Press, 1998), 8.

9. Jef Huysmans, "Post-Cold War Implosion and Globalisation: Liberalism Running Past Itself?" *Millennium: Journal of International Studies* 24, 3 (1995): 481.

10. Hoffmann, "The Crisis of Liberal Internationalism," 165.

11. Ibid., 175.

12. Antonio Franceschet and David Long, "Taking Liberalism Seriously: Liberal International Theory in an Age of Globalization," paper presented to the 41st Annual International Studies Association Meetings, Los Angeles, March 14–18, 2000.

13. Cecelia Lynch, "The Promise and Problems of Internationalism," *Global Governance: a Review of Multilateralism and International Organizations* 5, 1 (1999): 84.

14. E. H. Carr, *The Twenty Years' Crisis* (Edinburgh: R&R Clark, 1942), 81–112.

15. Ibid., 54–80.

16. Ibid., 185.

17. Ibid., 139, 220.

18. Ibid., 111, 178.

19. Ibid., 69, 94, 100ff.

20. Ibid., 214–215.

21. Ibid., 244–245.

22. Ibid., 272.

23. Ibid., chap. 13.

24. David A. Welch, *Justice and the Genesis of War* (Cambridge: Cambridge University Press, 1993), 20.

25. Ibid., 19, emphasis in original.

26. Ibid., 210.

27. As he states, the "justice motive is an explanatory concept," ibid., 187.

28. Ibid., 193.

29. Hedley Bull, *The Anarchical Society: a Study of Order in World Politics* (London: Macmillan, 1977). See also Hedley Bull, "The State's Positive Role in World Affairs," *Daedelus* 108, 4 (1979): 111–123.

30. Terry Nardin, *Law, Morality and the Relations of States* (Princeton: Princeton University Press, 1983), 19.

31. Ibid., 20.

32. On this theme, see James N. Rosenau and Ernst-Otto Czempiel, eds., *Governance Without Government: Order and Change in World Politics* (Cambridge: Cambridge University Press, 1992).

33. Chris Brown, "Review Article: Theories of International Justice," *British Journal of Political Science* 27, 2 (1997): 274.
34. Nardin, *Law, Morality,* 90.
35. Ibid., 85. See also K. J. Holsti, "Governance without Government: Polyarchy in Nineteenth Century European International Politics," in *Governance without Government,* ed. Rosenau and Czempiel, 30–57.
36. Welch, *Justice and the Genesis of War,* 212–214.
37. Bull, "The State's Positive Role"; Nardin, *Law, Morality,* 47; Welch, *Justice and the Genesis of War,* 211.
38. Welch, 192.
39. Ibid., 199.
40. Ibid., 205.
41. Ibid., 208.
42. Nardin, *Law, Morality,* 255.
43. Ibid., 261.
44. Ibid., 47.
45. Ibid., 52.
46. Richard Devetak and Richard Higgott, "Justice Unbound? Globalization, States, and the Transformation of the Social Bond," *International Affairs* 75, 3 (1999): 485.
47. Mark MacKinnon, "Activists study how to stop free trade pact," *The Globe and Mail* (Toronto), January 27, 2001, A19.
48. See Andrew Moravcsik, "Taking Preferences Seriously: A Liberal Theory of International Politics," *International Organization* 51, 4 (1997): 513–555.
49. Nardin, *Law, Morality,* 239.
50. Ibid., 270.
51. Welch claims that international justice can be coherent only with reference to recognized norms by which to justify claims, *Justice and the Genesis of War,* 197.
52. Roland Robertson, *Globalization: Social Theory and Global Culture* (London: Sage, 1992). As Robert W. Cox notes, "Internationalization refers to changes affecting states and should be differentiated from globalization, which is a broader concept that refers to the whole range of activities and practices involving state and nonstate actors that tend toward a more integrated global system," in "An Alternative Approach to Multilateralism in the Twenty First Century," *Global Governance: A Review of Multilateralism and International Organizations* 3, 1 (1997): 106.
53. Craig N. Murphy, *International Organization and Industrial Change: Global Governance since 1850* (New York: Oxford University Press, 1994).
54. This bias also exists in John Rawls, *The Law of Peoples* (Cambridge: Harvard University Press, 1999).
55. See James N. Rosenau, "Towards an Ontology for Global Governance," in *Approaches to Global Governance Theory,* ed. Martin Hewson and Timothy J. Sinclair (Albany: State University of New York Press, 1999), 281–301, and James N. Rosenau, "Governance for the Twenty First Century," *Global*

Governance: A Review of Multilateralism and International Organizations 1, 1 (1995): 13–43.

56. Rosenau, "Towards an Ontology," 287.

57. Rosenau, "Governance for the Twenty First Century," 13–14.

58. Rosenau, "Towards an Ontology," 292.

59. Rosenau, "Governance for the Twenty First Century," 13.

60. Ibid., 14.

61. Ibid., 15.

62. Ibid., 16.

63. Rosenau, "Towards an Ontology," 297.

64. Craig N. Murphy, "Global Governance: Poorly Done and Poorly Understood," *International Affairs* 76, 4 (2000): 780–803.

65. Devetak and Higgott, "Justice Unbound?" 485.

66. Rosenau, "Governance in the Twenty First Century," 13f., 18.

67. Ibid., 18.

68. See for example Michael Walzer, "The Moral Standing of States: A Response to Four Critics," *Philosophy and Public Affairs* 9, 3 (1980): 209–229, and, more recently, Robert H. Jackson, *The Global Covenant: Human Conduct in a World of States* (Oxford: Oxford University Press, 2000).

69. See Tom Keating, "The United Nations and NATO's War: The Fallout from Kosovo," in *Adapting the United Nations to a Postmodern Era: Lessons Learned,* ed. W. Andy Knight (Basingstoke, UK: Palgrave, 2001), 178–190.

70. Richard Falk, "The Pursuit of International Justice: Present Dilemmas and an Imagined Future," *Journal of International Affairs* 52, 2 (1999): 421.

Chapter 6 Popular Sovereignty or Cosmopolitan Democracy? The Futures of Liberal Internationalism

1. Stanley Hoffmann, "The Crisis of Liberal Internationalism," *Foreign Policy* 98 (1995): 175–176.

2. MM, 1/14.

3. MM, 239/31.

4. Thomas W. Pogge, "Kant's Theory of Justice," *Kant-Studien* 79, 4 (1988): 413.

5. PP, 119.

6. Steve Chan, "In Search of the Democratic Peace: Problems and Promise," *Mershon International Studies Review* 41, 1 (1997): 64.

7. Ibid., 85.

8. Doyle, "Kant, Liberal Legacies and Foreign Affairs," in *Debating the Democratic Peace,* ed. Michael E. Brown, Sean M. Lynn-Jones, and Steven E. Miller (Cambridge: MIT Press, 1996), 3–57. See also Michael W. Doyle, "Liberalism and World Politics," *American Political Science Review* 80, 4 (1986): 1153–1169.

9. Russett, *Grasping the Democratic Peace: Principles of a Post-Cold War World* (Princeton: Princeton University Press, 1993), 4.

10. Charles W. Kegley Jr., "The Neoliberal Challenge to Realist Theories of World Politics: An Introduction," in *Controversies in International Politics: Realism and the Neoliberal Challenge*, ed. Charles W. Kegley Jr. (New York: St. Martin's Press, 1995), 9–10.

11. Russett, *Grasping the Democratic Peace*, 9–11.

12. Chan, "In Search of the Democratic Peace," 59.

13. Michael Cox, "Wilsonianism Resurgent? The Clinton Administration and the Promotion of Democracy," in *American Democracy Promotion: Impulses, Strategies, and Impacts*, ed. Michael Cox, G. John Ikenberry, and Takashi Inoguchi (Oxford: Oxford University Press, 2000), 230–231.

14. Russett, *Grasping the Democratic Peace*, 9.

15. Doyle, *Ways of War and Peace: Realism, Liberalism, and Socialism* (New York: W. W. Norton & Company, 1997), 206, 211; Russett, *Grasping the Democratic Peace*, 24. Cf. Waltz, *Theory of International Politics* (Reading, Mass: Addison-Wesley, 1979).

16. Christopher Layne, "Kant or Cant: the Myth of the Democratic Peace," in *Debating the Democratic Peace*, ed. Michael E. Brown, Sean M. Lynn-Jones, and Steven E. Miller (Cambridge: MIT Press, 1996), 159, 190.

17. Raymond Cohen, "Pacific Unions: A Reappraisal of the Theory That 'Democracies Do Not Go to War with Each Other,'" *Review of International Studies* 20, 3 (1994): 207–233.

18. Chan, "In Search of the Democratic Peace," 63.

19. Russett, *Grasping the Democratic Peace*, 11; see also John M. Owen, "How Liberalism Produces the Democratic Peace," *International Security* 19, 2 (1994): 87–125.

20. Cf. Scott Gates, Torbjørn Knutson, and Jonathan W. Moses, "Democracy and Peace: A More Skeptical View," *Journal of Peace Research* 33, 1 (1996): 1–10.

21. Owen, "How Liberalism Produces the Democratic Peace," 88 n. 8, 94.

22. Gates et al., "Democracy and Peace," 6.

23. Russett, *Grasping the Democratic Peace*, 4.

24. Ibid., 24.

25. Doyle, "Liberalism and World Politics," 1158, and Doyle, *Ways of War and Peace*, 252.

26. Russett, *Grasping the Democratic Peace*, 41, emphasis added.

27. Chris Brown, "'Really Existing Liberalism' and International Order," *Millennium* 21, 3 (1992): 313–328; John MacMillan, "A Kantian Protest Against the Peculiar Discourse of Inter-Liberal State Peace," *Millennium* 24, 3 (1995): 549–562.

28. Gates et al., "Democracy and Peace," 3.

29. Doyle, "Kant, Liberal Legacies and Foreign Affairs," 5, emphasis added.

30. Ibid.; cf. Russett, *Grasping the Democratic Peace*, 31.

31 PP, 100.

32. PP, 100.

33. Pierre Laberge, "Kant on Justice and the Law of Nations," in *International Society: Diverse Ethical Perspectives*, ed. David R. Mapel and Terry Nardin (Princeton: Princeton University Press, 1998); Otfried Höffe, "'Even a Nation

of Devils Needs the State': The Dilemma of Natural Justice," in *Essays on Kant's Political Philosophy*, ed. Howard Williams (Cardiff: University of Wales Press, 1992), 120–142.

34. Doyle, *Ways of War and Peace,* 257.
35. Russett, *Grasping the Democratic Peace,* 15.
36. Chan, "In Search of the Democratic Peace," 66.
37. UH, 41–53; QE, 54–60.
38. Doyle, "Kant, Liberal Legacies and Foreign Affairs," 54.
39. David Held, *Models of Democracy* (Stanford: Stanford University Press, 1987), 289.
40. David Held, *Democracy and the Global Order: From the Modern State to Cosmopolitan Governance* (Stanford: Stanford University Press, 1995).
41. Daniele Archibugi, "Models of International Organization in Perpetual Peace Projects," *Review of International Studies* 18, 4 (1992): 295–317; Archibugi, "From the United Nations to Cosmopolitan Democracy," in *Cosmopolitan Democracy: An Agenda for a New World Order,* ed. Daniele Archibugi and David Held (Cambridge, UK: Polity Press, 1995), 121–162; Andrew Linklater, "Citizenship and Sovereignty in the Post-Westphalian State," *European Journal of International Relations* 2, 1 (1996): 77–103; and Linklater, *The Transformation of Community: the Ethical Foundations of the Post-Westphalian Era* (Cambridge, UK: Polity Press, 1998). See the contributions to Daniele Archibugi, David Held, and Martin Köhler, eds., *Re-imagining Political Community: Studies in Cosmopolitan Democracy* (Stanford: Stanford University Press, 1998).
42. This is so especially without an agenda to democratize global politics; see Daniele Archibugi, "So What if Democracies Don't Fight Each Other?" *Peace Review* 9, 3 (1997): 379–384.
43. Daniele Archibugi and David Held, "Editors' Introduction," in *Cosmopolitan Democracy,* ed. Archibugi and Held, 3.
44. Held, *Democracy and the Global Order,* 267; see also Linklater, *The Transformation of Community,* 31.
45. Archibugi and Held, "Editor's Introduction," 4–5.
46. Ibid., 5.
47. Cf. Alan James, *Sovereign Statehood: The Basis of International Society* (London: George Allen & Unwin, 1986).
48. The distinction between a state's formal sovereignty and actual autonomy in international affairs is made by, among others, Mark W. Zacher, "The Decaying Pillars of the Westphalian Temple: Implications for International Order and Governance," in *Governance Without Government: Order and Change in World Politics,* ed. James N. Rosenau and Ernst-Otto Czempiel (Cambridge: Cambridge University Press, 1992), 61–62.
49. Held, *Democracy and the Global Order,* 253.
50. Cf. Hoffmann, "The Crisis of Liberal Internationalism."
51 Held, *Democracy and the Global Order,* 260–261.
52. Zacher, "The Decaying Pillars of the Westphalian Temple," 61–62.
53. Archibugi and Held, "Editors' Introduction," 5.

54. Held, *Democracy and the Global Order,* 267.
55. Ibid., 226.
56. Ibid., xi.
57. Archibugi and Held, "Editors' Introduction," 8–9.
58. Ibid. and Held, *Democracy and the Global Order,* 230.
59. Held, *Democracy and the Global Order,* 233.
60. Archibugi and Held, "Editors' Introduction," 14.
61. Maxwell A. Cameron, Robert J. Lawson, and Brian W. Tomlin, eds., *To Walk without Fear: The Global Movement to Ban Landmines* (Toronto: Oxford University Press, 1998), and Antonio Franceschet and W. Andy Knight, "International(ist) Citizenship: Canada and the International Criminal Court," *Canadian Foreign Policy* 8, 2 (2001): 51–74.
62. Held, *Democracy and the Global Order,* 234, emphasis in original.
63. Although the CD model is not, of course, "functionalist" like Mitrany's system.
64. Archibugi and Held, "Editors' Introduction," 9; see also Archibugi, "Models of International Organization," 295.
65. Linklater, *The Transformation of Community,* 174.
66. MM, 350–351/119–120.
67. Held, *Democracy and the Global Order,* 231.
68. PP, 113.
69. Held, *Democracy and the Global Order,* 230.
70. Ibid., 233, emphasis added.
71. A prominent example is Onora O'Neill, "Transnational Justice," in *Political Theory Today,* ed. David Held (Cambridge, UK: Polity Press, 1991), 279–310.
72. Laberge, "Kant on Justice and the Law of Nations," 88.
73. See Pogge, "Kant's Theory of Justice." Cf. Linklater, *The Transformation of Community,* 312.
74. Bartelson, "The Trial of Judgment," 255–279.
75. PP, 105–106.
76. PP, 106; see Daniele Archibugi, "Immanuel Kant, Cosmopolitan Law and Peace," *European Journal of International Relations* 1, 4 (1995): 429–456.
77. Archibugi, "Models of International Organization," 312.
78. Nicholas Greenwood Onuf, *The Republican Legacy in International Thought* (Cambridge: Cambridge University Press, 1998), 243.
79. Archibugi, "Models of International Organization," 314. Compare this to Held, who states that the problem is that Kant did not "elaborate adequately the conditions of such [universal] hospitality" that cosmopolitan law encompasses, *Democracy and the Global Order,* 228 and also 223.
80. On this distinction, see Thomas W. Pogge, "Cosmopolitanism and Sovereignty," *Ethics* 103, 1 (1992): 48–72. Archibugi has shed important light on this in "Immanuel Kant, Cosmopolitan Law and Peace," 450–451.
81. Onuf, *The Republican Legacy,* 241 n. 93.
82. James Bohman and Matthias Lutz-Bachman, "Introduction," in *Perpetual Peace: Essays on Kant's Cosmopolitan Ideal,* ed. James Bohman and Lutz-Bachman (Cambridge: MIT Press, 1997), 8–10.

Conclusion

1. Thomas W. Pogge, "Kant's Theory of Justice," *Kant-Studien* 79, 4 (1988): 412.
2. Ibid., 414.
3. Ibid., 415.
4. Ibid., 424.
5. On the contractarian elements of Kant's international thought, see Andrew Linklater, *Men and Citizens in the Theory of International Relations* (London: Macmillan, 1982), chap. 6.
6. Nicholas Greenwood Onuf, *The Republican Legacy in International Thought* (Cambridge: Cambridge University Press, 1998).
7. Linklater, *Men and Citizens,* 47.
8. Pogge, "Kant's Theory of Justice," 431.
9. Ibid., 433.
10. Ibid.

Works Cited

Archibugi, Daniele. "Models of International Organization in Perpetual Peace Projects." *Review of International Studies* 18, 4 (1992): 295–317.

Archibugi, Daniele. "Immanuel Kant, Cosmopolitan Law and Peace." *European Journal of International Relations* 1, 4 (1995): 429–456.

Archibugi, Daniele. "From the United Nations to Cosmopolitan Democracy." In *Cosmopolitan Democracy: an Agenda for a New World Order,* ed. Daniele Archibugi and David Held, 121–162. Cambridge, UK: Polity Press, 1995.

Archibugi, Daniele. "So What if Democracies Don't Fight Each Other?" *Peace Review* 9, 3 (1997): 378–384.

Archibugi, Daniele. "Cosmopolitical Democracy." *New Left Review* Second Series, 4 (2000): 137–150.

Archibugi, Daniele and David Held. "Editors' Introduction." In *Cosmopolitan Democracy: An Agenda for a New World Order,* ed. Daniele Archibugi and David Held, 1–16. Cambridge, UK: Polity Press, 1995.

Archibugi, Daniele, David Held and Martin Köhler, eds. *Re-imagining Political Community: Studies in Cosmopolitan Democracy.* Stanford: Stanford University Press.

Arendt, Hannah. *Lectures on Kant's Political Philosophy,* ed. Ronald Beiner. Chicago: University of Chicago Press, 1982.

Aristotle. *The Politics.* Toronto: Penguin Books, 1992.

Aristotle. *The Ethics.* Toronto: Penguin Books, 1993.

Ashley, Richard K. "Untying the Sovereign State: A Double Reading of the Anarchy Problematique." *Millennium: Journal of International Studies* 17, 2 (1988): 227–62.

Ashworth, Lucien M. and David Long, eds. *New Perspectives on International Functionalism.* Basingstoke, UK: Macmillan, 1999.

Axworthy, Lloyd. "Kosovo and the Human Security Agenda." Notes for an Address by the Honorable Lloyd Axworthy to the Woodrow Wilson School of Public and International Relations. Princeton University, 7 April 1999.

Baldwin, David A., ed. *Neorealism and Neoliberalism: the Contemporary Debate.* New York: Columbia University Press, 1993.

Bartelson, Jens. "The Trial of Judgment: A Note on Kant and the Paradoxes of Internationalism." *International Studies Quarterly* 39, 2 (1995): 255–279.

Bartelson, Jens. *A Genealogy of Sovereignty*. Cambridge: Cambridge University Press, 1995.

Berlin, Isaiah. *Four Essays on Liberty*. Oxford: Oxford University Press, 1969.

Bohman, James and Matthias Lutz-Bachman. "Introduction." In *Perpetual Peace: Essays on Kant's Cosmopolitan Ideal*, ed. James Bohman and Matthias Lutz-Bachman, 1–22. Cambridge: MIT Press, 1997.

Booth, William James. *Interpreting the World: Kant's Philosophy of History and Politics*. Toronto: University of Toronto Press, 1986.

Brown, Chris. " 'Really Existing Liberalism' and International Order." *Millennium: Journal of International Studies* 21, 3 (1992): 313–328.

Brown, Chris. "Review Article: Theories of International Justice." *British Journal of Political Science* 27, 2 (1997): 279–297.

Brown, Michael E., Sean M. Lynn-Jones and Steven A. Miller, eds. *Debating the Democratic Peace*. Cambridge: MIT Press, 1996.

Bull, Hedley. *The Anarchical Society: A Study of Order in World Politics*. London: Macmillan, 1977.

Bull, Hedley. "The State's Positive Role in World Affairs." *Daedalus* 108, 4 (1979): 111–123.

Cameron, Maxwell A., Robert J. Lawson, and Brian W. Tomlin, eds. *To Walk Without Fear: The Global Movement to Ban Landmines*. Toronto: Oxford University Press, 1998.

Carnois, Bernard. *The Coherence of Kant's Doctrine of Freedom*. Translated David Booth. Chicago: University of Chicago Press, 1987.

Carr, E. H. *The Twenty Years' Crisis*. Edinburgh: R&R Clark, 1942.

Cavallar, Georg. *Kant and the Theory and Practice of International Right*. Cardiff: University of Wales Press, 1999.

Chan, Steve. "In Search of the Democratic Peace: Problems and Promise." *Mershon International Studies Review* 41 (1997): 59–91.

Claude Jr., Inis L. *Swords Into Plowshares: The Problems and Progress of International Organization*. 4th ed. New York: Random House, 1984.

Cohen, Raymond. "Pacific Unions: A Reappraisal of the Theory That 'Democracies Do Not Go to War with Each Other.' " *Review of International Studies* 20, 3 (1994): 207–223.

Cox, Michael. "Wilsonianism Resurgent? The Clinton Administration and the Promotion of Democracy." In *American Democracy Promotion: Impulses, Strategies, and Impacts*, ed. Michael Cox, G. John Ikenberry, and Takashi Inoguchi, 218–239. Oxford: Oxford University Press, 2000.

Cox, Robert W. "Social Forces, States, and World Orders: Beyond International Relations Theory." In *Neorealism and its Critics*, ed. Robert O. Keohane, 204–254. New York: Columbia University Press, 1986.

Cox, Robert W. "An Alternative Approach to Multilateralism in the Twenty First Century." *Global Governance: a Review of Multilateralism and International Organizations* 3, 1 (1997): 103–116.

Devetak, Richard and Richard Higgott. "Justice Unbound? Globalization, States, and the Transformation of the Social Bond." *International Affairs* 75, 3 (1999): 483–498.

Doyle, Michael W. "Liberalism and World Politics." *American Political Science Review* 80, 4 (1986): 1153–1169.

Doyle, Michael W. "Kant, Liberal Legacies, and Foreign Affairs." In *Debating the Democratic Peace*, ed. Michael E. Brown, Sean M. Lynn-Jones, and Steven E. Miller, 3–57. Cambridge: MIT Press, 1996.

Doyle, Michael W. *Ways of War and Peace: Realism, Liberalism and Socialism.* New York: W. W. Norton & Company, 1997.

Falk, Richard. "The Pursuit of International Justice: Present Dilemmas and an Imagined Future." *Journal of International Affairs* 52, 2 (1999): 409–441.

Franceschet, Antonio and W. Andy Knight. "International(ist) Citizenship: Canada and the International Criminal Court." *Canadian Foreign Policy* 8, 2 (2001): 51–74.

Franceschet, Antonio and David Long. "Taking Liberalism Seriously: Liberal International Theory in an Age of Globalization." Paper presented to the 41st International Studies Association Meetings. Los Angeles. March 14–18, 2000.

Franke, Mark F. N. *Global Limits: Immanuel Kant, International Relations, and Critique in World Politics.* Albany: State University of New York Press, 2001.

Freeden, Michael. *New Liberalism: an Ideology of Social Reform.* Oxford: Clarendon Press, 1978.

Friedrich, Carl Joachim. *Inevitable Peace.* Cambridge: Harvard University Press, 1948.

Fukuyama, Francis. *The End of History and the Last Man.* New York: Avon Books, 1992.

Galston, William. "What is Living and What is Dead in Kant's Practical Philosophy." In *Kant and Political Philosophy: The Contemporary Legacy,* ed. Ronald Beiner and William James Booth, 207–233. New Haven: Yale University Press, 1993.

Gates, Scott, Torbjørn Knutson, and Johnathan W. Moses. "Democracy and Peace: a More Skeptical View." *Journal of Peace Research* 33, 1 (1996): 1–10.

Goldmann, Kjell. *The Logic of Internationalism: Coercion and Accommodation.* London: Routledge, 1994.

Gray, John. "Introduction." In *Conceptions of Liberty in Political Philosophy,* ed. Zbigniew Pelczynski and John Gray, 1–6. London: The Athlone Press, 1984.

Gray, John. *Liberalism.* 2nd ed. Minneapolis: University of Minnesota Press, 1995.

Haas, Ernst. *Beyond the Nation-State.* Stanford: Stanford University Press, 1964.

Halliday, Fred. "Three Concepts of Internationalism." *International Affairs* 64, 2 (1988): 187–198.

Hassner, Pierre. "Beyond Nationalism and Internationalism: Ethnicity and the World Order." *Survival* 35, 2 (1993): 51–77.

Hegel, G. W. F. *The Philosophy of Right.* Trans. T. M. Knox. Oxford: Oxford University Press, 1967.

Held, David. *Models of Democracy.* Stanford: Stanford University Press, 1987.

Held, David. "Cosmopolitan Democracy and the Global Order: Reflections on the 200th Anniversary of Kant's 'Perpetual Peace.'" *Alternatives* 20, 4 (1995): 415–429.

Held, David. *Democracy and the Global Order: From the Modern State to Cosmopolitan Governance*. Stanford: Stanford University Press, 1995.

Hemleben, John Sylvester. *Plans for World Peace through Six Centuries*. New York: Garland Publishing Co., 1943.

Hinsley, F. H. *Power and the Pursuit of Peace: Theory and Practice in the History of Relations among States*. Cambridge: Cambridge University Press, 1963.

Hinsley, F. H. *Sovereignty*. 2nd ed. Cambridge: Cambridge University Press, 1986.

Hobbes, Thomas. *Leviathan*. Toronto: Penguin Books, 1986.

Höffe, Otfried. " 'Even a Nation of Devils Needs the State: the Dilemma of Natural Justice.' " In *Essays on Kant's Political Philosophy*, ed. Howard Williams, 120–142. Cardiff: University of Wales Press, 1992.

Höffe, Otfried. *Immanuel Kant*. Translated Marshall Farrier. Albany: State University of New York Press, 1994.

Hoffmann, Stanley. *Duties beyond Borders: On the Limits and Possibilities of Ethical International Politics*. Syracuse: Syracuse University Press, 1981.

Hoffmann, Stanley. *Janus and Minerva: Essays on the Theory and Practice of International Politics*. Boulder: Westview Press, 1987.

Hoffmann, Stanley. "The Crisis of Liberal Internationalism." *Foreign Policy* 98 (1995): 159–177.

Holsti, K. J. "Governance without Government: Polyarchy in Nineteenth Century European International Politics." In *Governance without Government: Order and Change in World Politics*, ed. James N. Rosenau and Ernst-Otto Czempiel, 30–57. Cambridge: Cambridge University Press, 1992.

Huntington, Samuel P. *The Third Wave: Democratization in the Late Twentieth Century*. Norman: University of Oklahoma Press, 1991.

Hutchings, Kimberly. *Kant, Critique and Politics*. London: Routledge, 1996.

Huysmans, Jef. "Post-Cold War Implosion and Globalisation: Liberalism Running Past Itself?" *Millennium: Journal of International Studies* 24, 3 (1995): 471–87.

Jackson, Robert H. *The Global Covenant: Human Conduct in a World of States*. Oxford: Oxford University Press, 2000.

Jahn, Beate. "One Step Forward: Two Steps Back: Critical Theory as the Latest Edition of Liberal Idealism." *Millennium: Journal of International Studies* 27, 3 (1998): 613–641.

James, Alan. *Sovereign Statehood: the Basis of International Society*. London: Allen & Unwin, 1986.

Judah, Tim. *Kosovo: War and Revenge*. New York: Yale University Press, 2000.

Kant, Immanuel. *Religion within the Limits of Reason Alone*. Translated T. M. Greene and H. H. Hudson. New York: Harper & Row, 1960.

Kant, Immanuel. *Groundwork of the Metaphysic of Morals*. Trans. by H. J. Paton. New York: Harpertorch Books, 1964.

Kant, Immanuel. *Critique of Judgment*. Trans. by Werner S. Pluhar. Indianapolis and Cambridge: Hackett Publishing Company Inc., 1987.

Kant, Immanuel. "Idea for a Universal History With a Cosmopolitan Purpose." In *Kant's Political Writings*, ed. Hans Reiss, trans. by H. B. Nisbet, 41–53. Cambridge: Cambridge University Press, 1991.

Kant, Immanuel. "An Answer to the Question: 'What is Enlightenment.'" In Kant's Political Writings, ed. Hans Reiss, trans. H. B. Nisbet, 54–60. Cambridge: Cambridge University Press, 1991.

Kant, Immanuel. "On the Common Saying: 'This May be True in Theory, But it Does Not Apply in Practice.'" In *Kant's Political Writings*, ed. Hans Reiss, trans. H. B. Nisbet, 61–92. Cambridge: Cambridge University Press, 1991.

Kant, Immanuel. "Perpetual Peace: a Philosophical Sketch." In *Kant's Political Writings*, ed. Hans Reiss, trans. H. B. Nisbet, 93–130. Cambridge: Cambridge University Press, 1991.

Kant, Immanuel. "The Contest of the Faculties." In *Kant's Political Writings*, ed. Hans Reiss, trans. H. B. Nisbet, 176–190. Cambridge: Cambridge University Press, 1991.

Kant, Immanuel. "Conjectures on the Beginning of Human History." In *Kant's Political Writings*, ed. Hans Reiss, trans. H. B. Nisbet, 221–234. Cambridge: Cambridge University Press, 1991.

Kant, Immanuel. *Critique of Practical Reason*. Trans. Lewis White Beck. Saddle River, N.J.: Prentice Hall/Library of Liberal Arts, 1993.

Kant, Immanuel. *Critique of Pure Reason*. Trans. Werner S. Pluhar. Indianapolis and Cambridge: Hackett Publishing Company Inc., 1996.

Kant, Immanuel. *The Metaphysics of Morals*. Trans. Mary J. Gregor. Cambridge: Cambridge University Press, 1996.

Keating, Tom. "The United Nations and NATO's War: the Fallout from Kosovo." In *Adapting the United Nations to a Postmodern Era: Lessons Learned*, ed. W. Andy Knight, 178–190. Basingstoke, UK: Palgrave, 2001.

Kedourie, Elie. *Nationalism*. 4th ed. Oxford: Basil Blackwell Inc., 1983.

Kegley, Charles W. Jr. "The Neoliberal Challenge to Realist Theories of World Politics: An Introduction." In *Controversies in International Politics: Realism and the Neoliberal Challenge*, ed. Charles W. Kegley Jr., 1–14. New York: St. Martin's Press, 1995.

Kelly, George Armstrong. *Idealism, Politics and History: Sources of Hegelian Thought*. Cambridge: Cambridge University Press, 1969.

Keohane, Robert O. "International Liberalism Reconsidered." In *The Economic Limits to Modern Politics*, ed. John Dunn, 165–194. Cambridge: Cambridge University Press.

Knippenberg, Joseph. "The Politics of Kant's Philosophy." In *Kant and Political Philosophy: The Contemporary Legacy*, ed. Ronald Beiner and William James Booth, 155–172. New Haven: Yale University Press, 1993.

Laberge, Pierre. "Kant on Justice and the Law of Nations." In *International Society: Diverse Ethical Perspectives*, ed. David R. Mapel and Terry Nardin, 83–102. Princeton: Princeton University Press, 1998.

Layne, Christopher. "Kant or Cant: the Myth of the Democratic Peace." In *Debating the Democratic Peace*, ed. Michael E. Brown, Sean M. Lynn-Jones, and Steven E. Miller, 157–201. Cambridge: The MIT Press, 1996.

Levy, Jack S. "Domestic Politics and War." In *The Origin and Prevention of Major Wars*, ed. R. I. Rotberg and T. K. Rabb, 81–99. Cambridge: Cambridge University Press, 1989.

Linklater, Andrew. *Men and Citizens in the Theory of International Relations.* London: Macmillan, 1982.

Linklater, Andrew. *Beyond Realism and Marxism: Critical Theory and International Relations.* London: Macmillan, 1990.

Linklater, Andrew. "The Problem of Community in International Relations." *Alternatives* 15, 2 (1990): 135–153.

Linklater, Andrew. "The Question of the Next Stage in International Relations: a Critical-Theoretical Point of View." *Millennium: Journal of International Studies* 21, 1 (1992): 77–98.

Linklater, Andrew. "Citizenship and Sovereignty in the Post-Westphalian State." *European Journal of International Relations* 2, 1 (1996): 77–103.

Linklater, Andrew. *The Transformation of Community: the Ethical Foundations of the Post-Westphalian Era.* Cambridge, UK: Polity Press, 1998.

Locke, John. *Second Treatise of Government.* Indianapolis: Hackett Publishing Company, 1980.

Long, David. "The Harvard School of Liberal International Theory: a Case for Closure." *Millennium: Journal of International Studies* 24, 3 (1995): 489–505.

Long, David. "Conclusion: Inter-War Idealism, Liberal Internationalism, and Contemporary International Theory." In *Thinkers of the Twenty Years' Crisis: Inter-War Idealism Reassessed,* ed. David Long and Peter Wilson, 302–328. Oxford: Clarendon Press, 1995.

Lynch, Cecelia. "The Promise and Problems of Internationalism." *Global Governance: a Review of Multilateralism and International Organization* 5, 1 (1999): 83–101.

Machiavelli, Niccolò. *The Prince.* Trans. by Harvey C. Mansfield Jr. Chicago: University of Chicago Press, 1985.

MacMillan, John. "A Kantian Protest against the Peculiar Discourse of Inter-Liberal State Peace." *Millennium: Journal of International Studies* 24, 3 (1995): 549–562.

MacMillan, John. "Democracies Don't Fight: A Case of the Wrong Research Agenda." *Review of International Studies* 22, 4 (1996): 275–299.

Matthew, Richard A. and Mark W. Zacher. "Liberal International Theory: Common Threads, Divergent Strands." In *Controversies in International Politics: Realism and the Neoliberal Challenge,* ed. Charles W. Kegley Jr., 107–150. New York: St. Martin's Press, 1995.

Meadowcroft, James. "Introduction." In *The Liberal Political Tradition: Contemporary Reappraisals,* ed. James Meadowcroft, 1–12. Cheltenham, UK: Edward Elgar, 1996.

Mitrany, David. *A Working Peace System.* Chicago: Quadrangle Books, 1966.

Moravcsik, Andrew. "Taking Preferences Seriously: A Liberal Theory of International Politics." *International Organization* 51, 4 (1997): 513–553.

Mulholland, Leslie Arthur. *Kant's System of Rights.* New York: Columbia University Press, 1990.

Murphy, Craig N. *International Organization and Industrial Change: Global Governance since 1850.* New York: Oxford University Press, 1994.

Murphy, Craig N. "Global Governance: Poorly Done and Poorly Understood." *International Affairs* 76, 4 (2000): 780–803.

Nardin, Terry. *Law, Morality and the Relations among States*. Princeton: Princeton University Press, 1983.

Nicholson, Peter. "Kant on the Duty Never to Resist the Sovereign." *Ethics* 86, 3 (1976): 214–230.

O'Brien, Robert and Anne Marie Goetz, Jan Aart Scholte, Mark Williams, eds. *Contesting Global Governance: Multilateral Economic Institutions and Global Social Movements*. Cambridge: Cambridge University Press, 2000.

O'Neill, Onora. *Constructions of Reason*. Cambridge: Cambridge University Press, 1989.

O'Neill, Onora. "Transnational Justice." In *Political Theory Today*, ed. David Held, 279–310. Cambridge, UK: Polity Press, 1991.

Onuf, Nicholas Greenwood. *The Republican Legacy in International Thought*. Cambridge: Cambridge University Press, 1998.

Owen, John M. "How Liberalism Produces Democratic Peace." *International Security* 19, 2 (1994): 87–125.

Pentland, Charles. *Integration Theory and European Integration*. London: Faber and Faber, 1973.

Robertson, Roland. *Globalization: Social Theory and Global Culture*. London: Sage, 1992.

Pogge, Thomas W. "Kant's Theory of Justice." *Kant-Studien* 79, 4 (1988): 407–433.

Pogge, Thomas W. *Realizing Rawls*. Ithaca: Cornell University Press, 1989.

Pogge, Thomas W. "Cosmopolitanism and Sovereignty." *Ethics* 103, 1 (1992): 48–72.

Pogge, Thomas W. "Is Kant's Rechtslehre Comprehensive?" *The Southern Journal of Philosophy* 36, Supplement (1997): 161–187.

Rawls, John. *A Law of Peoples*. Cambridge: Harvard University Press, 1999.

Richardson, James L. "Contending Liberalisms: Past and Present." *European Journal of International Relations* 3, 1 (1997): 5–33.

Richardson, James L. *Contending Liberalisms in World Politics: Ideology and Power*. Boulder: Lynne Rienner Publishers, 2001.

Riley, Patrick. *Kant's Political Philosophy*. Totowa, NJ: Rowman and Littlefield, 1983.

Riley, Patrick. "Elements of Kant's Practical Philosophy." In *Kant and Political Philosophy: The Contemporary Legacy*, ed. Ronald Beiner and William James Booth, 9–37. New Haven: Yale University Press, 1993.

Robinson, William I. *Promoting Polyarchy: Globalization, US Intervention and Hegemony*. Cambridge: Cambridge University Press.

Rosen, Allen D. *Kant's Theory of Justice*. Ithaca: Cornell University Press, 1993.

Rosenau, James N. "Governance in the Twenty First Century." *Global Governance: a Review of Multilateralism and International Organization* 1, 1 (1995): 13–43.

Rosenau, James N. *Along the Domestic–Foreign Frontier: Exploring Governance in a Turbulent World*. Cambridge: Cambridge University Press, 1997.

Rosenau, James N. "Towards and Ontology for Global Governance." In *Approaches to Global Governance Theory,* ed. Martin Hewson and Timothy J. Sinclair, 287–301. Albany: State University of New York Press, 1999.

Rosenau, James N. and Ernst-Otto Czempiel, eds. *Governance without Government: Order and Change in World Politics.* Cambridge: Cambridge University Press, 1992.

Rousseau, Jean-Jacques. *The First and Second Discourses.* Ed. Roger D. Masters, trans. Roger D. Masters and Judith R. Masters. New York: St. Martin's Press, 1964.

Rousseau. Jean-Jacques. *The Social Contract.* Trans. G. D. H. Cole. London: Everyman's Library, 1986.

Russett, Bruce. *Grasping the Democratic Peace: Principles of a Post-Cold War World.* Princeton: Princeton University Press, 1993.

Schmidt, Brian C. *The Political Discourse of Anarchy: a Disciplinary History of International Relations.* Albany: State University of New York Press, 1998.

Shell, Susan Meld. *The Rights of Reason: A Study of Kant's Philosophy and Politics.* Toronto: University of Toronto Press, 1980.

Shell, Susan Meld. "Kant's Political Cosmology: Freedom and Desire in the 'Remarks' Concerning Observations on the Feeling of the Beautiful and the Sublime." In *Essays on Kant's Political Philosophy,* ed. Howard Williams, 81–119. Cardiff: University of Wales Press, 1992.

Skinner, Quentin. "Meaning and Understanding in the History of Ideas." In *Meaning and Context: Quentin Skinner and His Critics,* ed. James Tully, 29–67. Cambridge: Polity Press, 1988.

Smith, Michael Joseph. "Liberalism and International Reform." In *Traditions of International Ethics,* ed. Terry Nardin and David R. Mapel, 201–224. Cambridge: Cambridge University Press, 1992.

Suganami, Hidemi. "Reflections on the Domestic Analogy: The Case of Bull, Beitz and Linklater." *Review of International Studies* 12, 2 (1986): 145–158.

Suganami, Hidemi. *The Domestic Analogy in World Order Proposals.* Cambridge: Cambridge University Press, 1989.

Taylor, Charles. "Kant's Theory of Freedom." In *Conceptions of Liberty in Political Philosophy,* ed. Zbigniew Pelczynski and John Gray, 100–122. London: Althone Press, 1984.

Tesón, Fernando. "Kantian International Liberalism." In *International Society: Diverse Ethical Perspectives,* ed. David R. Mapel and Terry Nardin, 103–113. Princeton: Princeton University Press, 1998.

Tuck, Richard. *The Rights of War and Peace: Political Thought and International Order from Grotius to Kant.* Oxford: Oxford University Press, 1999.

Velkey, Richard. *Freedom and the Ends of Reason: On the Moral Foundation of Kant's Critical Philosophy.* Chicago: University of Chicago Press, 1989.

Walker, R. B. J. *Inside/Outside: International Relations as Political Theory.* Cambridge: Cambridge University Press, 1993.

Waltz, Kenneth N. *Theory of International Politics.* Reading, Mass.: Addison-Wesley, 1979.

Waltz, Kenneth N. "Kant, la démocratie e la paix." In *L'année 1795: Kant, Essai Sur La Paix,* ed. Pierre Laberge, Guy Lafrance and Denis Dumais, 187–213. Paris: Librairie J. Vrin, 1997.

Walzer, Michael. "The Moral Standing of States: a Response to Four Critics." *Philosophy and Public Affairs* 9, 3 (1980): 209–229.

Weber, Cynthia. *Simulating Sovereignty: Intervention, the State, and Symbolic Exchange.* Cambridge: Cambridge University Press, 1995.

Welch, David A. *Justice and the Genesis of War.* Cambridge: Cambridge University Press, 1993.

White Beck, Lewis. "Kant's Two Conceptions of the Will in Their Political Context." In *Kant and Political Philosophy: The Contemporary Legacy,* ed. Ronald Beiner and William James Booth, 38–49. New Haven: Yale University Press, 1993.

Wight, Martin. "Why Is There No International Theory?" In *Diplomatic Investigations,* ed. Herbert Butterfield and Martin Wight, 17–34. London: George Allen & Unwin, 1966.

Wight, Martin. *International Theory: The Three Traditions.* London: Leicester University Press, 1991.

Williams, Howard. *Kant's Political Philosophy.* Oxford: Basil Blackwell, 1983.

Williams, Howard, ed. *Essays on Kant's Political Philosophy.* Cardiff: University of Wales Press, 1992.

Wilson, Peter. "Introduction." In *Thinkers of the Twenty Years' Crisis: Inter-War Idealism Reassessed,* ed. David Long and Peter Wilson, 2–14. Oxford: Clarendon Press, 1995.

Zacher, Mark W. "The Decaying Pillars of the Westphalian Temple: Implications for International Order and Governance." In *Governance without Government: Order and Change in World Politics,* ed. James N. Rosenau and Ernst-Otto Czempiel, 58–101. Cambridge: Cambridge University Press, 1992.

INDEX

anarchy
  among sovereign states, 44–5, 49,
    51, 55, 56, 60–1, 77, 119
  lawlessness, 33, 38, 47, 48, 50–1, 55,
    73
autonomy, *see* freedom

Bentham, Jeremy, 73, 76, 117
Berlin, Isaiah, 24, 25–6

Carr, E. H., 71, 77, 86–7, 90–1, 94
  see also liberal internationalism;
    criticisms of
categorical imperative, 18, 24, 30,
    36–7, 48, 124
  see also morality
cold war, 2, 3
  post-cold war era, 74, 91, 108–9,
    114–5
confederalism, *see* federalism
Copernican hypothesis, 15–6
  see also epistemology
cosmopolitanism
  democratic form of, 113, 116–8, 119
  Kantian, 4, 5–6, 62, 65, 104, 120–1,
    127
critical philosophy, 4, 9–11, 14, 23
  see also epistemology

democracy
  Kant's views on, 60, 105
  pacific effects of, 60, 74, 108–9,
    112–3
  see also popular sovereignty
democratization, 2, 74, 103, 106, 109,
    114
"Doctrine of Right," *see Metaphysics of
    Morals, The*
Doyle, Michael W., 76–7, 80–2, 106,
    110

enlightenment
  Kantian principle, 39, 112, 119, 130
  epistemology, 14–5, 63
ethics, *see* morality

federalism
  Kant's views on, 45, 60–2, 118
freedom
  autonomy, 4, 20–1, 67, 113
  external form, 31–4, 51, 55, 57,
    120–4
  internal form, 29–31, 47, 105
  negative and positive versions, 24–5,
    64

global governance
  definition of, 98, 99–100
  democratic forms of, 5
globalization, 2, 86–8, 96, 98, 115, 129

Hegel, G. W. F., 30
Held, David, 113–4, 117
Hinsley, F. H., 46
history
  Kant's views of, 39, 45, 62–5, 77
  see also enlightenment; Kantian
    principle
Hobbes, Thomas, 14, 17, 19, 43, 69
Höffe, Otfried, 26
Hoffmann, Stanley, 87–9, 101, 103

international justice, 54, 57–8, 68, 96,
    102
  see also justice

justice
  Kant's views on, 5–7, 25–7, 31–4, 44,
    54, 104, 125
  theory of, 7, 92
  see also international justice